GW00691139

CORFU

Windrush Island Guides
include

LANZAROTE
MADEIRA and PORTO SANTO
MENORCA
MALTA, GOZO and COMINO

CORFU

Nigel Coleman and Conrad Mewton

THE WINDRUSH PRESS
GLOUCESTERSHIRE

Acknowledgements
The authors would like to thank Etana Jacobson for her enthusiastic assistance with research in Corfu, Lia Mathioudakis and the staff of the National Tourist Organisation of Greece in Corfu for their invaluable help and tireless answering of our questions, and Pippa Hughes for her friendly advice and encouragement. In addition thanks are due to Corfu residents Major John Forte and Mr and Mrs Leon Chaitow for their knowledgeable advice; to Ian Hepburn of the Royal Society for the Protection of Birds, Dee Darters for travel information and Andrew Johnson for his assistance with the section on sailing; also to the National Tourist Organisation of Greece in London.

First published in Great Britain by
The Windrush Press,
Windrush House,
Main Street,
Adlestrop, Moreton-in-Marsh,
Gloucestershire
1991

Text and photographs (except where otherwise shown)
© Nigel Coleman 1991

ALL RIGHTS RESERVED

British Library Cataloguing in Publication Data
Coleman, Nigel
    Corfu.
    1. Greece. Travel
    I. Title
    914.955

    ISBN 0-900075-07-4

Typeset by DP Photosetting, Aylesbury, Bucks
Printed and bound in Hong Kong by Paramount Printing Group Ltd

Cover illustrations: (front) Paleokastritsa Monastery
(back) Vatonies village

CONTENTS

Sports and Activities

For Margaret and John, without whose help this book could never have been completed

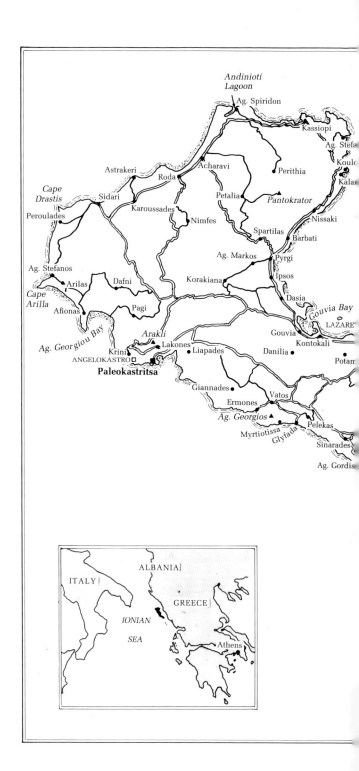

CORFU

0 1 2 3 miles 5

0 1 2 3 4 5 kms

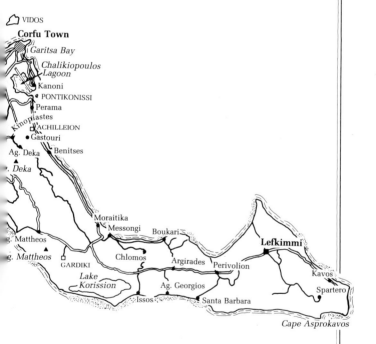

VIDOS

Corfu Town

Garitsa Bay

Chalikiopoulos
Lagoon

Kanoni

PONTIKONISSI

Perama

Kinopiastes

ACHILLEION

Gastouri

Ag. Deka

Benitses

. Deka

Moraitika

Messongi

Boukari

Lefkimmi

g. Mattheos

g. Mattheos

GARDIKI

Chlomos

Argirades

Perivolion

Kavos

Spartero

Lake
Korission

Ag. Georgios

Issos

Santa Barbara

Cape Asprokavos

INTRODUCTION

Corfu's image as a holiday destination has become some-what tarnished in recent years, and prejudice against the island has on occasion been unfairly fanned by lurid stories in the press. During the summer peak season, admittedly, there are a handful of beach resorts on the island which seem bent on attracting an element of Western European youth whose sole aim on holiday appears to be to drink to excess, to make as much noise as possible and to pick fights. But in truth this less than desirable aspect of Corfu is an aberration of which most visitors need scarcely be aware. This book is concerned to demonstrate that for the discerning holiday-maker Corfu is as tranquil, friendly and beautiful as it has always been, and to act as a guide to the 95 per cent of this lovely island which remains impervious to the more tawdry aspects of mass tourism.

A surprise among Greek islands, Corfu's limestone hills are clothed with green and its monumental olive trees grow to heights of 50 feet and more. In the mountainous interior of the north and the flatter regions of the southern part of the island the traditional pace of life remains untouched by tourism, the peaceful atmosphere of the many inland villages clustered around their picturesque churches mak-ing a sharp contrast to the brashness of the lively beach resorts nearby. Corfu's coastline (over 200 km of it) offers scores of glorious beaches, some highly developed for tourism while others remain unfrequented and unspoilt. An attractive blend of old-world timelessness, spectacular scenery and the international holiday scene contributes to the island's complex character.

Corfu Town, the capital and home to about a third of the population, offers gracious Venetian architecture, pictu-resque streets and a relaxed, Mediterranean style of life as well as exciting shopping. Here and all over the island can be traced the relics of one of the richest and most eventful histories it is possible to imagine. For British visitors, in particular, the legacy of the nineteenth-century British Protectorate offers fascinating glimpses of a more gracious past – including the possibility of watching a game of cricket.

Since ancient times Corfu has been beloved of poets, artists, writers and playwrights. Homer wrote of Corfu as

Away from the tourist resorts, the traditional Corfiot way of life still flourishes

the home of the magical Phaeacians, and Shakespeare is widely believed to have had Corfu in mind as the setting for *The Tempest*. Later the painter Edward Lear celebrated Corfu's natural beauty, while W. E. Gladstone claimed 'never to have witnessed such complete and contented idleness as at Corfu'. More recently still, Lawrence and Gerald Durrell have both left memorable testimonies to their time spent on the island.

Corfu has something to offer holidaymakers of all types. Outside the main tourist 'season', in spring, early summer and autumn, the countryside is alive with birdsong and resplendent with wild flowers, of which many thousands of species (some of them unique to Greece) can be seen: these are the seasons for the walker, the naturalist and the photographer. In high summer the beaches offer perfect swimming, sunbathing and watersports of all kinds. The bars and cafés stay open late, and there is music and dancing far into the night. The Corfiots are by nature a hospitable people, proud of their island and appreciative of its natural beauty. It is our hope that this guide will help visitors to find and enjoy the 'real Corfu' for themselves.

GETTING THERE

By Air

Most of Corfu's visitors arrive by air, and a large proportion of their flights are chartered by British tour operators. Charter flights without an accommodation package are organised by Cosmos, Falcon, Flair, Horizon, Manos, Olympic, Next Island, Skyworld, Thomson and Unijet. All these, and the package holidays, are bookable at travel agents anywhere in the UK, and most provincial airports handle Corfu flights.

Scheduled flights are with Olympic Airways from London Heathrow (tel: 081-745-7253). On Mondays throughout the summer these fly direct to Corfu (cheapest high season return fare £221): the flight duration is about four hours. All the year round there are scheduled flights via Athens costing, in July 1990, £320 return in summer and £307 return in winter. Athens to Corfu takes 45 minutes, there are 3 flights daily, and this element of the journey costs £94 return. Olympic Airways also fly from Zakynthos to Corfu on Wednesdays and Sundays. For reservations in Greece, contact a travel agent or the airline: in Athens, tel: 9616161; in Corfu, tel: 38695/6; in Zakynthos, tel: 28611.

CORFU AIRPORT

Corfu airport is remarkable for its situation. Built on land reclaimed from the Chalikiopoulos lagoon, 2 km south of Corfu Town on the Benitses road, the runway extends out into the water, ending below the tip of the Kanoni peninsula and only metres away from the pedestrian causeway between it and Perama. Planes pass alarmingly close to the Kanoni peninsula and the noise of the jet engines makes the ground and walls reverberate. Nevertheless, plane-spotting from Kanoni is a popular pastime and ensures good business for the Royal Hotel's balcony cafeteria.

The airport runway accommodates medium-sized jets; the terminal building is rather small and can become uncomfortably overcrowded when flights are delayed. In high summer the airport handles up to 25 international flights a day, the majority originating in the UK. The busiest day tends to be Monday.

Departure lounge, Corfu airport. There are plans to enlarge the facilities

Money changing facilities (open 09.00–23.00) and a post office can be found within the arrivals area; the departure zone includes a duty-free shop and a cafeteria.

There is no public bus service between the airport and the town but there are plentiful taxis (about 400 dr. to the town centre). Olympic Airways run a private bus which connects with their scheduled arrivals and departures. Tel. no. of airport: 30180.

By Sea

If you take your car from London to Corfu, the quickest route is thought to be: Ostend – Brussels – Stuttgart – Munich – Salzburg – Ljubljana – Belgrade – Thessaloniki – Athens – Patras – Igoumenitsa – Corfu. The distance involved is around 3255 km (1950 miles) and at least 50 hours driving time. As well as an international driving licence, drivers from the UK will need a Green Card extending their insurance policy to foreign countries and should ascertain the legal requirements as regards headlamp adjustment, spares carried, etc., of each of the countries on route. A ferry of Minoan Lines leaves Patras at 22.00, arriving in Corfu at 08.00; the reverse journey leaves Corfu at 22.00, arriving at Patras at 07.00. From Igoumenitsa there are 14 sailings a day in summer and nine in winter.

An alternative route by road from London is through France and Italy. Sailings from Ancona are at 14.00 (Anek-Cretan Maritime Line), 20.00 (Minoan Lines) and 21.00 (Strintzis Lines). All arrive in Corfu 22 hours later. In summer, the Strintzis ferry calls at Dubrovnik en route. From Brindisi, Hellenic Mediterranean Lines sail at 22.00, arriving in Corfu at 07.00 next day (return trip departs Corfu at 09.00, arriving in Brindisi at 17.00); Adriatica Line sail at 22.30, arriving Corfu at 07.00 (return: dep. Corfu 09.00, arrive Brindisi 17.00); Fragline leave Brindisi at 21.00, arr. Corfu 06.30 next day (return: dep. Corfu 08.30, arr. Brindisi 16.00).

The Yugoslavian ferry company, Jadrolinija, runs a year-round service between Split and Igoumenitsa for Corfu.

Travel agents will ascertain up to date fares, or the ferry companies can be contacted through their UK agents:

Minoan Lines, c/o P. & O. European Ferries, Channel House, Channel View Rd, Dover, Kent, CT17 9TJ. (tel: 0304-203388)

Anek-Cretan Maritime Line, c/o Viamare Travel Ltd, 33 Mapesbury Rd, London NW2 4HT. (tel: 081-452-8231)

Adriatica Line, c/o Sealink Travel Centre, P.O. Box 29, Victoria Station, London SW1 1JX. (tel: 071-828-1940)

Hellenic Mediterranean Lines, c/o Mediterranean Passenger Services Ltd, 9 Hanover St, London W1R 9HG. (tel: 071-499-0076)

Strintzis Lines, c/o Viamare Travel Ltd, as above.

Fragline, c/o Peco Tours, 52 Heath Rd, Caterham, Surrey. (tel: 0883-348511)

Jadrolinija, c/o Yugotours Ltd, Chesham House, 150 Regent St, London W1R 5FA. (tel: 071-341-7321)

There is a daily rail service from London Victoria to Brindisi, changing trains at Milan. It takes approximately 21 hours to Milan and 12 hours from Milan to Brindisi for the ferry connection to Corfu. The return fares in summer 1990 were £217 2nd class and £315 1st class.

Euroway (tel: 071-730-8235) run a coach to Athens which leaves London (Victoria Coach Station) on Tuesdays and Fridays at 20.00, arriving in Athens at 06.30 on the fourth day. The return journey is from Athens at 15.30, also on Tuesdays and Fridays, reaching London four days later at 07.30. The price in 1990 was £147 return. Coaches leave Athens (bus terminal: 100 Kifissou St) for Corfu via Igoumenitsa at 07.00 and 20.30, taking 11 hours. The 1990 fare was 2900 dr., not including the ferry.

Five cruise companies include Corfu in their itineraries:

Cunard Line Ltd, South-Western House, Canute Rd, Southampton, SO9 12A. (tel: 0703-634166)

Chandris Cruises Ltd, 5 St Helen's Place, London EC3A
6BJ. (tel: 071-588-2598)
Intercruise, Equity Cruises, 77/79 Great Eastern St,
London EC2A 2HU. (tel: 071-729-1929)
P. & O. Cruises, 77 New Oxford St, London WC1A
1PP. (tel: 071-831-1881)
Swan Hellenic Ltd, 77 New Oxford St, London WC1A
1PP. (tel: 071-831-1515).

TRAVEL ON CORFU

Maps

A legacy of Greece's insecure past is that it is still not possible to obtain accurate large scale maps of the country. Of the several touring maps of Corfu available, none can be wholeheartedly recommended, as they all fall down in the less populous areas of the island, marking non-existent roads, showing quite rough tracks as though they were asphalted modern roads, etc. The most reliable general-purpose maps are the Clyde Leisure version (available in UK bookshops, as is the Hallwag, which is in practice the

Wayside shrines of all types from the simplest to the most elaborate are a feature of Corfu's roads

same map) and the Freytag and Berndt map distributed on the island by the Efstathiadis Group in Athens. Both incorporate plans of Corfu Town and show contours together with the distances between main centres. (A detailed map of the town, with more street names and an index of the main sights, is available locally, published by Kimon Rappos.) An interesting, and surprisingly practical, alternative is the satellite map of Corfu published by Maptec International (available on the island); this is essentially a 1:70,000 satellite photograph of the island taken on a summer morning from a height of 832 km, on which roads and place names have subsequently been marked.

Car hire

The variety of sights and scenery on Corfu makes hiring a car an attractive option for those who want to see more of the island than just the tourist resorts. Despite the fact that, as in mainland Greece, car hire and petrol are by no means cheap, the majority of visitors to Corfu find this an irresistible way to explore this beautiful island, if only for a day or two.

As a rough guide, typical high season car hire rates in 1990 fell within the following range:

	dr. per day	3 days	7 days
small car (Subaru, Suzuki SS 40 or similar)	5200–6500	15500–18500	35000–42000
medium car (Datsun Cherry, Opel Corsa, VW Golf)	6000–7300	18000–22000	40000–50000
Open car (Daihatsu or Suzuki)	7400–9000	22000–27000	49000–60000
Suzuki Jeep	8900–12000	23000–32000	57000–72000

Value added tax (currently at 18 per cent) is added to the above rates. Although rentals of three days or more include unlimited mileage, for shorter hire periods only 100 km is usually included free, additional mileage being charged at between 30 and 60 dr. per km (plus tax). Insurance *is* included, but for full cover, including damage caused by the driver, a further 1000–2000 dr. (plus tax) per day can be paid for a collision damage waiver. It is important when hiring a car to establish clearly exactly what element of tax and insurance cover is included in the price being quoted. Delivery and collection is often free, but there may be a clause in the hire document excluding damage to tyres or the underside of the car caused by driving on unmade roads – a point worth remembering if you propose to leave the beaten track.

In general, car hire is only available to drivers aged over 23 who have held a licence for more than one year, though it may be possible to find exceptions to this rule. Strictly, an international driving permit is necessary, but in practice for EEC nationals a current national driving licence and a passport are all the documentation required. A deposit may be requested, but this is almost always waived if the hirer pays by credit card.

Car rental offices abound; even quite small tourist villages boast one, while in the larger resorts there are often several. In Corfu Town itself there are over a dozen, with familiar international firms well represented as well as Greek concerns. Many have offices at the airport and in the Xenofontos Stratigou/Old Port area.

Bicycles, Scooters and Motorcycles

Every year there are serious accidents involving visitors using hired two-wheeled transport on Corfu, and any number of minor ones – of which the number of crutches and bandaged limbs to be seen in the resorts provide all too visible evidence. The main reasons for this are the mechan-

Hiring a light motorcycle is one of the most popular ways to explore the island

ical unreliability of some of the machines rented, the inexperience of many riders, and the state of the minor roads – on which unexpected potholes, crumbling verges, sharp, poorly cambered bends and slippery patches of loose gravel can all catch the inexperienced unawares, particularly when two people are riding an underpowered machine.

Nevertheless, hiring a scooter or motorcycle is an ideal and inexpensive way to see the island at one's own pace. The golden rule is to shop around before hiring (and ideally be seen to be doing so): choose a firm whose bikes look reliable and well maintained; test the brakes and lights, and ensure the machine (usually Japanese) is powerful enough to take two of you if that is your intention (bearing in mind that many of the roads and tracks are steep, particularly in the north); avoid driving at night (many vehicles on Corfu are inadequately lit, and potholes and other road surface flaws are obviously particularly hazardous in the dark). Above all, check that your holiday insurance does not exclude injury sustained while riding a hired machine; if this is the case, take out extra insurance, ideally a policy which includes provision for an emergency flight home if necessary.

There are bike rental agencies in Corfu Town (particularly around the Old Port, along Arseniou St and in the major roads leading from San Rocco Square), and in all the main resorts. You will probably be required to show a passport (and maybe leave it as a surety), but for hiring motorcycles under 50 cc. neither a licence nor insurance is required by law. Rates vary considerably (another reason for being seen to shop around), and the price quoted may or may not include taxes and some sort of insurance; rates for longer periods should be lower than the basic daily rate. Crash helmets are not usually provided.

Bicycles can be also be hired in most towns and resorts, for around 500 dr. a day, and in many of the flatter parts of the island provide a pleasant means of exploring the immediate locality.

Driving on Corfu

The main roads on the island are all metalled and many are excellently maintained. Particularly in the mountainous north of Corfu, however, there can be dangerous rockfalls, especially after rain; other hazards in this area are the sharp bends, which are rarely signalled in advance and often poorly cambered. Secondary roads vary from the perfectly serviceable to precipitous rocky tracks down which it would be foolish to take an ordinary hired car. Corfu's roads are constantly being improved, however, the main roads being widened and fresh stretches of unmade surface metalled every year.

Road signs on main roads, when there are any, usually appear in both the Greek and the Roman alphabet, though there is sometimes a gap before the Roman sign appears. On minor roads, however, this is considerably less likely and it is worth looking up a few Greek traffic instructions in a phrase book before setting out. 'Give Way' signs are rare at junctions, so unless traffic from the right is quite obviously on a minor road or you can see that it is governed by a 'STOP' sign, it is safest to assume that it has priority. The speed limit on all the island's roads is 80 km.p.h. unless otherwise indicated. Since 1989, the wearing of seatbelts has been compulsory (though you might not divine this from observing local drivers), and the use of horns is forbidden in towns. The Greek Traffic Police impose rigorous penalties for speeding. In Corfu Town there is limited free parking around the Old Port and the Esplanade: illegal parking elsewhere results in a fine and, on occasion, the removal of your number plates.

ACCIDENTS

The innumerable small roadside shrines seen throughout Corfu were originally erected to protect lands and crops from bad spirits. Nowadays, however, they frequently commemorate the scene of a road accident and offer protection against a recurrence; keeping this is mind will prevent more accidents than any number of warning signs.

In the event of an accident it is advisable to exchange names and addresses and insurance details and inform the car hire agency immediately. Generally there is no requirement to inform the police unless someone has been hurt. In the event of a breakdown in your own car, the ELPA, (Automobile Touring Club of Greece) provides light repairs and other assistance free to members of other national motoring organisations. Their office is in the square by the Old Port, at Patriarchou Athinagora, Corfu (tel: 39504); in emergencies they can be contacted by telephoning 104 (24 hours).

PETROL

Petrol stations are easy to find near the main population centres, particularly in the north-east. Most close at 19.00, however, (having opened at 07.00) and almost all close on Sundays. (A rota ensures that there is always at least one petrol station open in the environs of Corfu Town on

Colourful *amaxa* passing the Palace of St Michael and St George, Corfu Town

Sundays and in the evenings – other garages should display a notice showing which it is.)

In Corfu Town itself there are three stations in the Av. Alexandras area between San Rocco Sq and Garitsa Bay, and several on Xen. Stratigou St (Mandouki road) and other main routes out of town. Similarly, they are plentiful on the main roads north and south as far as Dasia and Perama respectively. Elsewhere on the island petrol stations are usually well signposted (often from up to 2 km away). They can be found, for example, at or near Moraitika, Nissaki, Kassiopi, Agios Spiridon, Roda, Karoussades, Sidari, Armenades, Liapades, Vatos, the Messonghi bridge, Linia, Argirades, Perivolion, Lefkimmi and Kavos, with three more on the Corfu-Pelekas road. At the time of writing unleaded petrol was available at the BP Station near the New Port, at Lefkimmi and at Alikes Potamou.

Petrol prices are very much the same as in the UK.

Taxis

Taxis in Corfu Town are relatively easy to find: there are between 150 and 200 cabs and ranks at Methodiou St (nr San Rocco Sq., tel: (30383), G. Theotoki St (Pallas Cinema, tel: 39911), the Esplanade (tel: 39926), New Fortress Sq. (tel: 34124) and the Old Port (tel: 37933). Radio taxis can be summoned by dialling 33811, 33812 or 41333. Many taxi-drivers speak a little English and all have meters. Fares are, in theory at least, controlled and usually reasonable; between 01.00 and 05.00 drivers are entitled to charge double the rate shown on the meter. Outside the town, there are taxis in almost all of the resorts, at least in summer. For journeys over longer distances it is highly advisable to establish the price in advance.

Within Corfu Town an alternative to ordinary taxis is provided by the cheerfully painted horse-drawn victorias known as *carrozzas* or *amaxes*. The sunhatted horses are based in the square beside the Old Port: their usual route is to and from the Esplanade via the sea wall (where they seriously hold up the traffic on occasion), but they also go to the end of the Kanoni peninsula. Prices are controlled but not of course cheap, and worth negotiating in advance.

Buses

Corfu has an extremely extensive network of bus routes; fares are very reasonable, and travelling on the buses is a good way to experience Corfiot life. The main bus station in Corfu Town is in Plateia Neou Frouriou (New Fortress Square), near the Old Port; from here green and white buses leave for most of the island and also for the mainland (buses make the 11-hour journey to Athens from here twice a day). The numbers of the bus routes and departure times are displayed outside the bus company's offices at the southern corner (furthest from the fort). However, note that route numbers can change; also that from June onwards extra buses are gradually added to the more popular routes, and correspondingly withdrawn from mid-September. It is possible to obtain timetables from the bus station and from tourist offices, but on all but the most popular routes it is unwise to place full confidence in official timetables given out by the tourist authorities, or even worse, set out in guide books! In general it is safest when making a return trip to check both departure and return times at the bus station, ideally with the driver of the bus concerned. Buses to faraway corners of the island may depart very early in the morning, returning early afternoon, which may make planning a day trip complicated; they occasionally depart early, so it is sensible to arrive at the bus station in good time. On most routes the last bus departs at 19.00 or 20.00 and even on the most popular runs (from Ipsos/Pyrgi to Corfu, for example) the latest goes at 22.30.

Bus stops in the countryside are indicated by a KTEL *stasis* sign, sometimes with a shelter; buses going in either direction will stop at these signs if requested, and may indeed stop in other places if energetically signalled. Corfu buses can become extremely crowded, as would-be passengers are never turned away.

There are other bus stations in the town: the Esplanade is the terminus for the buses serving the town and its suburbs, such as Mandouki and Kanoni – services run about half-hourly until 22.45; from San Rocco Square blue buses leave for nearby destinations such as Benitses (via Perama), Tebloni (Potamos, Evropouli), Gastouri (for the Achilleion), Pelekas and Dasia (via Kontokali and Gouvia). The timetables for these routes are considerably less variable than those for the rural buses.

HOTELS AND RESTAURANTS

The great majority of visitors to Corfu are accommodated in villas, apartments or hotels in the coastal resorts. Independent travellers, however, may well prefer to stay in Corfu Town itself, which besides being an extremely attractive city offers the best eating out and shopping facilities and is the most convenient starting point for excursions to other parts of the island.

Hotels

The prices charged by Greek hotels are controlled by the NTOG, whose office can supply price lists (rates quoted normally include VAT but not national or local taxes). Hotels are classified into de luxe and grades A-E: *minimum* rates for a double room (1991) were: de luxe – 7940 dr., Category A – 5630, B – 3480, C – 2810, D – 2400, E – 2080 and tavernas – 1510; a 10 per cent surcharge may be imposed for an occupancy of less than 3 nights and 20 per cent for an extra bed in the room. These are minimum rates: the normal high season rate will obviously be considerably more – perhaps three or four times as much. By law a price list must be displayed in every room. A private bathroom is standard for grades de luxe, A and B, and is sometimes offered in category C: D and E hotels may well have only minimal bathrooms and uncertain hot water – they are also unlikely to have restaurants attached. The better grade of hotel is a *xenodocheion* in Greek: cheaper grades are known as *pandocheia*.

In addition to hotels, there are also bed and breakfast establishments (*pansiones*), also graded into categories and price-controlled; these usually offer better facilities than D and E category hotels. Some tavernas also offer simple accommodation – guests are usually expected to eat in, and the rooms may inevitably be somewhat noisy.

Finally, accommodation is available in private rooms, both officially licensed and otherwise. These exist in quantity all over the island and, except in the peak season, are quite easy to find – they are commonly advertised by rough and ready signs (which may read *domatia* or *enoikia-zontai domatia*) on or near the accommodation. Rooms in private houses are usually clean, comfortable and good value; guests share the home's facilities with the family, and staying in them makes an excellent introduction to Greek island life. Visitors arriving by ferry are likely to encounter a crowd of people on the quayside anxious to show them to a room in the family home – late in the day this option may well appeal to independent travellers, but do establish the price and whether hot water is available before you set off – also how far you have to walk! In general rooms might cost 1500–2500 dr. per night for a double in the summer.

During July and August most accommodation is, not surprisingly, fully booked. Travel agents and the NTOG can provide complete lists of hotels and the Tourist Police, based near the Tourist Office at the western end of the Palace of St Michael and St George in Corfu Town (tel: 30265), will assist in finding accommodation. In addition the Tourist Bureau at 43 Arseniou St (tel: 22101) offers a room-finding service – it is open from 08.00–13.00 and 16.00–19.00 every day in the season.

The following is a brief list of the main hotels. All are open from April to October inclusive and their telephone prefix is 0661, unless otherwise stated:

CORFU TOWN AND KANONI

De Luxe
Corfou Palace Hotel, Demokratias Ave. 115 rooms, overlooking Garitsa Bay; air cond., gardens, two swimming pools and a wide range of facilities (tel: 39485-7, fax: 31749)
Corfu Hilton International, Nafsicas St, Kanoni. 256 rooms, 4 km from Corfu Town (to which there is a complimentary bus service) overlooking Kanoni beach; gardens, indoor and outdoor swimming pools, health club, tennis courts, bowling, many other facilities; open all year (tel: 36540-4, fax: 36551)

Category A
Ariti, Kanoni. 174 rooms, air cond., heated swimming pool, (tel: 33885-7)
Cavalieri, 4 Kapodistriou St. 62 rooms, roof garden, open all year (tel: 39041, 39336)
Corfu Divani Palace, 20 Nafsikas St, Kanoni. 163 rooms, air cond., pool, disco (tel: 38996-8)

Category B
Arion, 5 Emm. Theotoki St, Anemomylos. 105 rooms, roof garden, pool, mini-golf; open all year (tel: 37950)
Astron, 15 Donzelot St. 33 rooms, heating, open all year (tel: 39505, 39986)

King Alkinoos, 20 Dim. Zafiropoulou St. 61 rooms, heating, open all year (tel: 39300-2, 31898)
Marina Beach Hotel, Mon Repos, Anemomylos. 102 rooms, air cond. (tel: 32783-5)
Olympic, 4 Meg. Doukissis Marias St. 50 rooms, heating, open all year (tel: 30532-4)

Category C
Arkadion, 44 Kapodistriou St (tel: 37670-2); **Atlantis**, Xen. Stratigou St (tel: 35560-2); **Bretagne**, 27 Georgaki St, Garitsa (tel: 30724); **Calypso**, 4 Vraila Armeni St (tel: 30723); **Dalia**, 9 Eth. Stadiou Sq. (tel: 32341); **Hermes**, 14 G. Markora St (tel: 39321); **Ionion**, 46 Xen. Stratigou St (tel: 39915); **Royal**, Kanoni (tel: 37512,35342-7); **Salvos**, Kanoni (tel: 30429, 37889)

Pensions
Anthis (B) (tel: 25804), Phoenix (B) (tel: 42290)

D and E Hotels
D – Acropole, Constantinoupolis, Europa, Metropolis, Nea York; E – Elpis, Karmen, Kriti, Kypros, Spilia.

NORTH-EAST

De Luxe
Astir Palace, Kommeno Bay. 308 rooms, air cond., tennis, pool, sauna, beauty salon (tel: 91481, 35108, 44300-5)
Kontokali Palace, Kontokali beach. 243 rooms on wooded peninsula, air cond., gardens, pool, entertainments programme, disco (tel: 38736-9)

Category A
Corcyra Beach Hotel, Gouvia Bay. 252 rooms, pools, tennis courts, squash, entertainments programme, disco (tel: 30770-2, fax: 91591)
Corfu Chandris, Dasia. 252 rooms, air cond., tennis, pool, complimentary bus to town (tel: 33871-5, 93351-4, fax: 93458)
Dassia Chandris, Dasia. 251 rooms, air cond., pool (tel: 33871-5, fax: 93458)
Elea Beach, Dasia. 198 rooms, pool, hairdresser (tel: 93490-3, fax: 93494)
Eva Palace, Dafnila. 132 rooms, air cond., tennis court, pool (tel: 91286, 91237, 37706)
Grecotel Daphnila Bay, Dafnila. 259 rooms, heated pool, floodlit tennis courts, shops, water sports (tel: 91520-3, fax: 91026)

Kerkyra Golf, Alikes Potamou. 246 rooms, pool, tennis, horseback riding, hairdresser, shops, night club, open Mar–Oct (tel: 31785-7, fax: 38120)
Margarona Palace, Dasia. 119 rooms, air cond., pool, tennis, night club, open all year (tel: 93742-6)
Nissaki Beach, Nissaki. 241 rooms, air cond., pool, tennis, mini-golf, shops, disco (tel: 91232-3)
Radovas, Kommeno. 116 rooms, air cond., pool (tel: 91218, 91342)

Category B
Acharavi Beach, Acharavi. 63 rooms, air cond., pool, tennis, open May–Oct (tel: 0663-93146, 93102, 93124)
Alexiou, Barbati. 52 rooms, air cond., pool, shops (tel: 0663-91383)
Ionian Princess, Ag. Pandeleimon, nr Acharavi. 90 rooms, pools, sports facilities, night club, open May–Oct (tel: 0663-93110-11)
Molfetta Beach, Gouvia. 23 rooms, air cond. (tel: 91915-9)
Paloma Bianca, Dasia. 34 rooms, pool (tel: 93406,93575-6)
Park, Gouvia. 184 rooms, pool (tel: 91310, 91347, fax: 91531)
Ypsos Beach, Ipsos. 60 rooms, pool (tel: 93232, 93247)

Category C
Alykes Beach, Alikes Potamou (tel: 31111); **Amalia**, Dasia (tel: 93520); **Artemis**, Gouvia (tel: 91509); **Barbati**, Barbati (tel: 93594); **Dassia**, Dasia (tel: 93224, 93268); **Elizabeth**, Gouvia (tel: 91451); **Feakion**, Gouvia (tel: 91264, 91497); **Galaxy**, Gouvia (tel: 91220-3); **Iliada**, Gouvia (tel: 91360); **Ionian Sea**, Ipsos (tel: 93241); **Marie**, Ag. Pandeleimon (tel: 0663-93106); **Mega**, Ipsos (tel: 93216, 93208); **Platanos**, Ipsos (tel: 93240); **Primavera**, Dasia (tel: 91911-3); **Pyrgi**, Pyrgi (tel: 93209); **Salina**, Alikes Potamou (tel: 36782); **Sun Flower**, Gouvia (tel: 91568); **Sunset**, Alikes Potamou (tel: 31203); **The Port**, Pyrgi (tel: 93293); **Tina**, Dasia (tel: 93664)

Pensions
Sofia (B), Dassia; Angela (B), Gouvia (tel: 91336); Villa Matella (A), Kalami

D and E Hotels
Triantafylia (D), Alikes Potamou; Kormoranos Beach (D), Acharavi; Scheria (D), Dasia; Hariklia, Louvre, Orfeas, Sirena (all D), Gouvia; Costas Beach (D), Ipsos; Oasis (D),

Kassiopi; Panorama (D), Aleka (E), Kontokali; Ionia, Theo (both D), Pyrgi.

NORTH-WEST

Category A
Akrotiri Beach, Paleokastritsa. 127 rooms, pool (tel: 0663-41275-7)

Elly Beach, Liapades beach. 48 rooms, open May–15 Oct (tel: 0663-41455)

Ermones Beach, Ermones. 272 rooms/bungalows, tennis, watersports (funicular to beach), pool, nearby golf (tel: 94241-2)

Grand Hotel, Glifada. 228 rooms, air cond., pool, complimentary buses to town and golf course (tel: 94201-2, 37919, 38574, 45100-6)

Category B
Glyfada Beach, Glifada. 35 rooms (tel: 94257-8)

Oceanis, Paleokastritsa. 67 rooms, pool, disco (tel: 0663-41230)

Paleokastritsa, Paleokastritsa. 165 rooms, night club (tel: 0663-41207, 41217)

Roda Beach, Roda. 359 rooms, heating, tennis, 3 pools, mini-golf, disco, open Mar–Oct (tel: 0663-93246, 93202)

Category C
Aphroditi Beach, Sidari (tel: 0663-31247); **Apollon**, Paleokastritsa (tel: 0663-41211, 41220); **Arilla Beach**, Arilas (tel: 0663-31401); **Astrakeri Beach**, Astrakeri (tel: 0663-31238); **Astoria**, Sidari (tel: 0663-31315); **Liapades Beach**, Liapades (tel: 0663-41294); **Marina**, Arilas (tel: 0663-31400); **Mimoza**, Sidari (tel: 0663-31363, 31361); **Odysseus**, Paleokastritsa (tel: 0663-41209); **Saint Stefanos**, Ag. Stefanos (W) (tel: 0663-31254); **Sidari Beach**, Sidari (tel: 0663-31115/6); **Silver Beach**, Roda (tel: 0663-93134); **Three Brothers**, Sidari (tel: 0663-31242); **Village Roda Inn**, Roda (tel: 0663-93358); **Vladimir**, Ag. Ioannis (tel: 52275)

Pension
Marida (A), Ag. Ioannis (tel: 52410)

D and E Hotels
Hermes, Zefiros (both D), Fivos, Paleo Inn (both E), Paleokastritsa; Ninos (E), Roda; Sidari (D), Sidari.

SOUTH

De Luxe
Miramare Beach, Moraitika. 142 rooms, tennis, mini-golf, shops, entertainments programme (tel: 30183, 30226-8, fax: 55305)

Category A
Aghios Gordis, Ag. Gordis. 199 rooms, tennis, pool, games room, sauna (tel: 0663-53320/1)

Alexandros, Perama. 76 rooms, air cond., pool, shops, disco (tel: 36855-7, 33160)

Apollo Palace, Messongi. 158 rooms, tennis, pool (tel: 55433, 55601)

Delfinia, Moraitika. 83 rooms (tel: 30318, 32279, 33045, 30224)

Regency, Benitses. 185 rooms, air cond., pool, sauna, shops, disco (tel: 92305-10, 92295)

San Stefano, Benitses. 250 rooms, air cond., tennis, pool, shops (tel: 36036, 92292-4)

Yaliskari Palace, nr Sinarades. 212 rooms, air cond., indoor and outdoor pools, tennis (tel: 31400)

Category B
Achilles, Benitses. 74 rooms, children's playground (tel: 92425-6, fax: 92436)

Aeolos Beach, Benitses. 231 rooms, pool, shops, disco (tel: 33132-4)

Akti Motel, Perama (tel: 30574)

Albatros, Moraitika. 53 rooms, pools (tel: 55315-7)

Belvedere, Tsaki nr Benitses. 170 rooms, pool, entertainments programme (tel: 92442, 92381)

Delfinakia, Moraitika. 81 rooms, tennis, pool (tel: 33045, 55451-2, fax: 55450)

Gemini, Messongi. 84 rooms, pool (tel: 55398, 55211-13)

Golden Sands, Ag. Georgios (S). 50 rooms, pool, children's playground (tel: 0662-51225)

Messonghi Beach, Messongi. 796 rooms, tennis, pools, shops, entertainments programme (tel: 38684-6, fax: 55334)

Montaniola, Gastouri. 58 rooms, air cond., pool (tel: 56205)

Oasis, Perama. 67 rooms, pool, disco (tel: 38190, 33120, 33173, fax: 25435)

Potomaki, Benitses. 150 rooms, pool, disco (tel: 30889, 92201)

Category C
Aegli, Perama (tel: 39812, 30610); **Argo**, Gastouri (tel:

39468); **Bella Vista**, Benitses (tel: 92087-8); **Boukari**, Boukari beach (N. of Argirades) (tel: 0662-22687); **Cavos**, Kavos (tel: 0662-22107); **Chrysses Folies**, Ag. Gordis (tel: 0663-30407); **Continental**, Perama (tel: 33113); **Corfu Maris**, Benitses (tel: 38684); **Fryni**, Perama (tel: 36877); **Loutrouvia**, Benitses (tel: 92258, 92342); **Margarita**, Moraitika (tel: 55267); **Maria House**, Messongi (tel·38684-6); **Melissa Beach**, Messongi (tel: 55229, 55264); **Pontikonissi**, Perama (tel: 36871-2); **Prasino Nissi**, Moraitika (tel: 55379); **Rossis**, Messongi (tel: 55352); **Roulis**, Messongi (tel: 55353); **Sea Bird**, Moraitika (tel: 92348); **Three Stars**, Moraitika (tel: 92457)

Pensions
Alonakia (B), Agios Gordis (tel: 0663-30407); El Greco (B), Gastouri (tel: 31893); Roussos (B), Kavos (tel: 0662-22122); Solonaki (B) and Fontana (D), Moraitika; Elvira (B), Potamos (S) (tel: 91587)

D and E Hotels
Agios Georgios (D), Agios Georgios; Diethnes (D), Pink Paradise (E), Agios Gordis; Avra, Benitsa (both D), Eros, Riviera (both E), Benitses; Cavo Palace Alexandria, Panela Beach (both D), Spyrou (E), Kavos; Moraitika (E), Moraitika; Perama (E), Perama

Camping

Camping is only permitted on official sites, which have running water, electricity and toilet facilities. Prices vary from around 300–600 dr. per person per day (children aged 3-10 half-price), plus about 500–900 dr. for site and car parking (or caravans). Tents can be hired at some sites and there may be small additional charges for electricity, use of hot water etc.

Corfu's sites are as follows:

Dasia: **Karda Beach** (tel: 93595): on the beach, 100 places, bar, supermarket. Open April–end October.
Dasia (Kormari): **Kormarie** (tel: 93587): inland, 100 places, bar, restaurant, supermarket. Open April–October.
Gouvia: **Dionyssos** (tel: 91417): on the beach, 88 places, bar, restaurant, supermarket, swimming pool. Open May–20 October.
Ipsos: **Ipsos Ideal** (tel: 93243,93588): inland, 92 places, bar, restaurant, supermarket. Open April–end October.
Ipsos: **Kerkira Camping** (tel: 93246, 93308, 93579): on the beach, bar, restaurant, supermarket. Open April–end October.

Karoussades: **Karoussades** (tel: 0663-31394): inland (nearest beach Astrakeri), 63 places, bar, restaurant, supermarket. Open April–October.

Kavadades: **St George** (tel: 0663-41254/41384): inland (nearest beaches Arilas, Ag. Georgiou Bay), 45 places, bar, restaurant, supermarket. Open April–end October.

Kontokali: **Kontokali Beach International** (tel: 91170, 91202): inland, 93 places, restaurant, supermarket. Open April–end October.

Messongi: **Ippokambos** (tel: 55364): inland, 70 places, bar, restaurant, supermarket, swimming pool. Open mid-April–mid-October.

Paleokastritsa: **Paleokastritsa** (tel: 0663-41204): inland, 107 places, bar, restaurant, supermarket. Open April–October.

Pyrgi: **Paradise** (tel: 93282, 93558): on the beach, 108 places, restaurant, supermarket. Open April–October.

Roda: **Roda Beach** (tel: 0663-93120/34761): inland, 83 places, bar, restaurant, supermarket, swimming pool. Open April–October.

Vatos (Chavares): **Pelekas Vatos** (tel: 94393): inland (nearest beach Pelekas), 37 places, bar, restaurant, supermarket. Open April–October.

Youth Hostel

There is a youth hostel in Kontokali (tel: 91202); it is strictly only for members but you can join the Association on the spot: price approx. 500 dr. per night.

FOOD AND DRINK

Corfiot Cuisine

Although predominantly Greek, Corfu's cooking does owe something to its long occupation by the Venetians, particularly a predilection for tomato and pasta dishes, both introduced from Italy. In general the food is less spicy than on the mainland of Greece, and marginally less oily – the excellent quality of Corfu's olive oil ensures that, as a cooking medium, its flavour is not intrusive. (Garlic and olive oil are thought to be the essential factors which contribute to the island having an exceptionally low incidence of heart disease.) Herbs are important in Corfiot recipes, particularly oregano (*rigani*), basil (*vasilikos*) and mint (*dyosmos*). In country districts herbal remedies are still widely used in preference to modern medicine.

The main meal is taken either during the early afternoon

Mirtiotissa, for Lawrence Durrell 'perhaps the loveliest beach in the world'

Campanula versicolor and Greek chamomile

(left) Wild snapdragon in May   (right) Acanthus growing by an old olive tree

(left) Larkspur growing wild above Paleokastritsa
(right) Swallowtail butterfly © *Eric and David Hosking*   (below) Scops owl © *Eric and David Hosking*

or after 9 p.m. It typically consists of one cooked dish – meat or fish slowly casseroled in water with vegetables; olive oil and lemon juice are often added before serving. This is accompanied by salad, *feta* cheese and bread; it may be preceded by a selection of *mezethes* (hors d'oeuvres) and followed by fruit. In restaurants, of course, less conventional combinations of Greek dishes, as well as international cooking, are available.

Pork, lamb, beef and chicken all feature in **meat** cookery. Some of the more usual dishes are: *arni* or *arnopita*: lamb or lamb pie; *kokoretsi*: spicy pork and garlic sausages, *kotopoulo*: chicken, casseroled or grilled; *moussaka*: minced lamb or beef layered with aurbergines and *béchamel* sauce; *pastitsada*: veal with tomato sauce and pasta; *pastitsio*: minced beef and macaroni layered with *béchamel* sauce and cheese; *sofrito*: steak or veal stewed with brandy, garlic, herbs and vinegar; *souvlakia*: kebabs which may be of pork, lamb or veal; *stifado*: hare or rabbit stewed with onions, tomatoes, vinegar and garlic.

Lamb is the meat held in highest esteem and is traditionally eaten at Easter.

The seas around Corfu teem with **fish** but it tends to be expensive at the table. The most highly priced is lobster (*astako*): if genuinely caught off the west coast of Corfu, this will be the spiny lobster (*Palinurus elephas*) whose meat is confined to the claws. Other fish to be found on menus are: *barbouni*, red mullet; *fangri*, sea bream; *chtapodi*, octopus – caught between May and October; *garides*, prawns; *kalamarakia*, baby squid – deep-fried as an appetiser; *kalamaria*, squid – sometimes baked with an onion, rice and herb stuffing; *kefalos*, grey mullet, farmed in the Korission and Andinioti lakes – the roe is sold as 'Greek caviar'; *lithroni*, sea bass – often caught with bread and cheese! *savrithia*, Spanish mackerel – caught off the islets to the north-west; *sinagrida*, red snapper; *xifias*, swordfish – meaty, dense and very filling.

Corfu's own composite fish recipe is *bourtheto*, a peppery stew made with fish (as available), garlic and tomatoes. It originates in the Mandouki area of Corfu Town and is probably best eaten there. *Kakavia* is the Greek version of *bouillabaisse* or fish soup.

Taramasalata, one of Greece's most famous dishes internationally, is a paste made with fish roe – traditionally that of the grey mullet from Lake Korission but in present times often from Icelandic cod – blended with bread, spring onions, olive oil and lemon juice. It was invented as a Lenten speciality – during the pre-Easter period the devout may not eat fish with backbones.

Vegetables constitute a very important part of the Corfiot diet, are grown in wide variety and used extensively in home cooking. Oddly, their appearance on restaurant menus is rare except in the form of salads. The growers bring their produce every morning, except on Sunday, to the vegetable market at the foot of the New Fortress. A wide selection includes, in season: *anginares*, globe artichokes, grown in the south of the island; *angouria*, cucumber; *domates*, tomatoes, always ripened out of doors – the Corfiots prefer them slightly over-ripe, often split by the sun; *fassolakia freska*, french beans; *kolokithia*, courgettes; *kremithia*, onions; *lachano*, cabbage; *melitzanes*, aubergines; *patates*, potatoes; *rathikia*, dandelion leaves – these are a popular salad ingredient and cultivated for the purpose; *spanaki*, spinach.

These vegetables, together with pulses which are also sold widely, form the basis of many delicious vegetarian recipes which are detailed in *Greek Vegetarian Cooking* by the Corfiot writer, Alkmini Chaitow. All are simple to follow and use ingredients produced on the island. In truly rural areas people gather wild vegetables (*chorta*) with which they make pies (*chortapitta*).

As in the rest of Greece, *mezethes* (**hors d'oeuvres**) are served with drinks or eaten as a light meal. The most famous of these are: *anginares*: globe artichokes stewed with onions, herbs, garlic and lemon juice; *dolmades*: stuffed vine or cabbage leaves – the filling may be minced meat or a mixture of rice, onions and pine kernels; *domatosalata*: tomato salad – sliced tomatoes and olives, dressed with olive oil, vinegar and oregano; *choriatiki*: Greek salad – cubed *feta* cheese with tomatoes, cucumber, green peppers, lettuce, onions and olives; *hummus*: a paste of tahini, chick-peas, olive oil and garlic eaten on bread; *tzatziki*: yogurt, garlic and cucumber dip, also eaten on bread, which originates in the Lebanon.

Every village in Corfu has a multitude of **fruit** trees and very little fruit has to be imported. Apples, apricots, cherries, peaches, damsons, pears, figs, lemons and pome-granates all flourish. Wild strawberries (*fraoules*) are an island speciality. True oranges are not grown commercially, but the kumquat (*Citrus japonica*), a miniature orange, is an important and very Corfiot fruit. The London Horticultural Society introduced the tree from Japan in the nineteenth century; its cultivation was a great success and a thriving industry of liqueur-making has grown up. The fruits are also sold preserved in jars of syrup or, crystallised, in boxes: all three presentations are marketed to tourists as souvenirs of the island. Coach trips visit the factory and showroom of Mavromatis on the Paleokastritsa road; independent shoppers are also welcome (see p.106).

Nut-bearing trees include the almond, walnut, chestnut and hazel, all of which contribute to the local cuisine. *Soumada* is an almond drink taken diluted with water. Almonds and walnuts are widely used in cakes, desserts and sweets. The people of Corfu, in common with most other Greeks, like *patisserie*. *Baklavas* are probably the best known example: envelopes of pastry filled with nuts and honey, they are also popular in Turkey and the USSR. Other sweet concoctions are *kataifi*, a syrupy pastry with the texture of shredded wheat; *kourabiethes*, shortbread; *loukoumathes*, cinnamon and honey fritters; and *mandolato*, almond and honey nougat.

The very thin light pastry known as *fyllo* is a Greek speciality; it is tricky to make and is usually bought ready-made these days. Greek honey (*meli*) is excellent and may be offered with yogurt for breakfast.

Feta **cheese**, white and crumbly and an essential ingredient of the Greek salad, may be made from the milk of sheep or goats; the best comes from Epirus. A hard and salty sheep's milk cheese, *kefalotiri*, is used for grating on to pasta (like Parmesan); *graviera* is reminiscent of Swiss Gruyère.

The coffee house (*kafeneion*) is the traditional meeting place for Corfiot men, where they play cards, smoke, drink, strike business deals and discuss politics. Greek **coffee** (*kafe*) is made from ground African coffee beans boiled with water and sugar in a waisted 'saucepan' called a *briki*. It is served with a glass of water and may be *sketo* (without sugar and very bitter), *metrio* (medium sweet) or *gliko* (very sweet). Not all visitors enjoy the strength of *kafe* and should in that case ask for *nes*, which is instant coffee but not necessarily Nescafé: for white coffee ask for *nes me gala*. Tea is *tsai* and will be served without milk unless you ask for it (when it is likely to be evaporated). Water (*nero*) is safe to drink but bottled water probably tastes better. It is more easily obtainable uncarbonated. Brands include Loutraki, Nigita and Sariza.

Ginger beer, brought to Corfu by the British in the nineteenth century, became adopted as *tsitsibira* and remained extremely popular as a Corfiot drink until the 1930s. Since then it has been largely supplanted by Coca-Cola and other international fizzy drinks. It is still obtainable from a few outlets, however.

Among alcoholic drinks, **beer** (*bira*) is of the lager type and Northern European brands made under licence in Greece are the most widely available varieties. Sold in half-litre bottles, beer is cheaper than in the UK; draught beer, in contrast, tends to be more expensive. *Ouzo* is a famous Greek aperitif made from crushed grape stems; it tastes of aniseed and is deceptively potent: hence the custom of an accompanying glass of water, which may be added to the drink. *Retsina*, also very well known, is drunk more by visitors than locals: this is a white wine flavoured with pine resin and is definitely an acquired taste. Its aficionados say that it counterbalances the oiliness of Greek food. Sundry liqueurs are available, many with a kumquat base and produced by the island distilleries. The basic kumquat liqueur is cloyingly sweet and luridly orange; there are many derivatives in different colours and flavours. Good brandy, Metaxa being the most ubiquitous, and cheap gin add to a wide choice of alcoholic beverages.

Corfu's **wine** (*krasi*) industry is very old. The island's wines were celebrated in classical Greece and under the Angevins (1267–1386) vineyards were enlarged and planted with *monemvasia* vines whose grapes produce 'malmsey', the sweet red wine which features more than once in Shakespeare. The Venetians' encouragement of olive production dealt a deathblow to the industry and today the majority of wines offered on menus are from other islands or the mainland of Greece. Although Corfiot wine is not stocked by all restaurants it is worth seeking out; as it does not travel well, it is inadvisable to regard it as a souvenir to bring home. 'Coryfo' is the most usual label and may be red (*kokkino*) or white (*aspro*) – the dry white, served well chilled, is a refreshing, Sancerre-like wine, whose mild

Vineyard, southern Corfu: the wines of Corcyra were famous in classical Greece

Olives awaiting collection by the road. Under the Venetians the islanders were encouraged to plant olive trees on every spare corner of their land

flavour belies its alcoholic content. 'Paloumbi' from Sinarades is a pleasantly dry white; sweet whites are made in Lefkimmi and Petalia (Capo Bianco). Very small amounts of wine are produced from the vineyards of Makrades, Krini, Pagi, Strinilas and Chlomos and are only sold locally. Many households make their own wine and also vinegar.

Olive Oil

Corfu's venerable olive trees, some 500 years old, generate some of the best 'extra virgin' oil in the Mediterranean; even since the rise of tourism its production has retained great economic importance for the island (see pp.77-8). Bottles containing locally produced oil always have 'Kerkyra' on the label; such oil is golden and fresh-tasting because the olives are only pressed when ripe.

Corfu oil is the basis of much of the island's cuisine and olives preserved in brine are eaten as a nourishing snack. According to James Chatto and W.L. Martin's book, *A Kitchen in Corfu*, babies are christened with it, fishermen clarify shallow waters with it and builders add it to whitewash to prevent the whiteness rubbing off when touched. It is also used as a digestive aid, a skin moisturiser and an ingredient for an anti-rheumatism ointment.

Restaurants

Corfu offers a bewildering choice of places to eat, from basic beach bars to luxury restaurants. Eating places may have one of a number of names: generally speaking, a *psistaria* is a self-service or take away grill; a *taverna* is a family-run establishment serving local fare at reasonable prices, sometimes with accompanying entertainment; and an *estiatorio* is a restaurant which may be medium-priced or *de luxe*. Food is also served in a *zacharoplasteion*, basically a patisserie-cum-café. In all but the most expensive international restaurants, prices are controlled by the Tourist Police who make spot checks throughout the season.

It is generally cheaper to eat out in Corfu than in the UK. Two prices for each dish are shown on most menus: the higher of these is the one you pay, as it includes taxes and a service charge. It is usual, though not obligatory, to leave a 5 per cent–10 per cent tip. Service in Corfiot restaurants can be slow. Almost certainly you will be given bread at the beginning of a meal but this should not be put on the bill unless it is eaten; when there is a long wait for the first course, however, diners often find themselves unable to resist! It is wise not to order the whole meal at once as this may result in all the courses being brought simultaneously, cooling all the while.

Menus are invariably full of choice but do not vary in content much from one restaurant to another. Translations into English (sometimes with hilarious results) are always given: in tourist areas English is often the first language shown. All the well known specialities of Greece are available: *moussaka* is probably better ordered at lunchtime when it is freshly made. Uniquely Corfiot dishes, described

Discussing the menu in a beach restaurant, north-eastern Corfu

on pp.22–4, should be sought out as should the local wine. It is also easy to find international staples such as chips, hamburgers, steaks, etc. A fondness for Italian food dates from the Venetian occupation but now also pleases the large influx of tourists from Italy; pasta is an ingredient of several Corfiot recipes and Italian dishes are featured on most menus. Nowadays there are also many *pizzerias* on the island. The price of fish tends to be disproportionately high, since the fishing industry is in decline (many former fishing boats are now used for pleasure trips), and much of the catch is sent to Athens. If you order fish, you will be charged by weight and you may be invited to the kitchen to choose what should be cooked.

Local people eat a late lunch but most restaurants are open from noon for tourists; similarly, dinner can be taken from early evening until well past midnight according to taste. Many establishments, particularly those in beach resorts, are only open from May until October.

A limited selection of eating places follows:

CORFU TOWN

Apayio, 47 Eth. Antistasis (New Port): candle-lit rustic interior; up-market menu including a good selection of seafood; home-made cakes (tel: 43136).

Argo, Eth. Antistasis (New Port): excellent fresh fish and lobster; expensive (tel: 24398).

Averof, 4 Prosalendou St/Alipiou St: just inland from the Old Port, this old-established and well-known restaurant is in a narrow street crowded with tables out of doors; extremely busy – partly due to a tireless tout who 'invites' you in as you are browsing; good value and wide choice; Corfiot house wine (tel: 31468).

Corfou Palace Grill Room, Corfou Palace Hotel, Vas. Konstantinou (Garitsa Bay): cuisine claims to be French but is rather disappointing; high class surroundings, live music, expensive. Open 20.00–23.00 (tel: 39485).

Crêperie Asterix, Dousmani St (up steps from E. end of Filellinon St): snacks, sweet and savoury pancakes, salads, etc.

Meli Café, 30 Alexandras Ave: patisserie/café with small restaurant area at rear, interesting menu, good for a light snack; clean, modern 'ice cream parlour' ambience, but intrusive canned music; open 10.00–14.00, 17.30–23.00.

Orestes, 78 Xen. Stratigou St, New Port: Meals served indoors or in the garden; specialises in fresh fish, seafood and authentic Greek cuisine (tel: 35664).

Pantheon, 16 Prosalendou St: right opposite the Averof

Venetian wellhead in Kremasti Square

and its arch-rival, also employing a highly persuasive young man touting for custom; traditional Greek food, cheerfully scruffy ambience, reasonable prices (tel: 30921).

Pizza Pete's, Arseniou St; tourist-trap pizzeria on the sea wall with glorious views of Vidos and north-east coast, open 10.00–01.00.

Port, 36 El. Venizelou St: friendly restaurant with seating beside the harbour where smaller boats moor; fresh *sofrito*, *bourtheto* and locally caught fish. The waiters have a particularly perilous journey when bringing food to your table as the main port road separates the kitchen from the dining area. Very reasonable; open 06.00–03.00 (tel: 30921/42862).

Rex, 6 Kapidistriou St: directly behind the Liston, this unpretentious busy restaurant serves medium-priced Greek and Corfiot food; brisk service.

Venetian Well Bistro, Kremasti Square (up steps from Ag. Theodoras St near cathedral): unbeatable for both ambience and the originality of the cuisine. There is no printed menu, just a small selection of unusual and imaginative dishes which changes daily and is lovingly described to you by the courteous and multi-lingual staff. Tables outside stand beside a well-preserved Venetian well in a quiet square where swallows wheel overhead and two of the least mangy cats on Corfu prowl beguilingly around; the interior is decorated in traditional Corfiot style with modern frescoes. Service discreetly attentive; imaginative selection of wines from all over Greece, about which the staff are happy to give knowledgeable advice. Prices compare most favourably with more run-of-the-mill establishments in the town. Without doubt *the* outstanding restaurant in Corfu. Open 18.00–01.30, closed Mondays (tel: 44761).

Xenikhtis, 12 Potamou St: on the main road out of town towards Paleokastritsa, this 'gourmet' restaurant has an intimate ambience and attentive service; Greek, French and Italian dishes; children's menu; occasional live music. Open 19.00–02.00 except Sundays (tel: 24911).

THE NORTH-EAST

Palia Lefka, Alikes Potamou, 3km north of Corfu Town: on the main road by the river; offers Corfiot and international fare; Greek dancing nightly; open 'all day every day' (tel: 24618).

Mandarin Palace Chinese Restaurant, Kontokali: boasting four chefs and an extensive menu of Cantonese dishes, this restaurant enjoys a good reputation as well as magnificent views to Albania from its spacious terrace; rather expensive. Open 12.00–16.00 and 18.00–01.00 (tel: 71319/39159).

Pipilas, Kontokali: old-established restaurant claiming the late King Paul and Queen Frederika of Greece among its former patrons; good Greek cuisine and comprehensive wine list. Open 12.30–16.00 and 17.30–23.30. (tel: 91201).

Bella Mamma, Gouvia: friendly atmosphere, reasonable prices.

Komeno, Kommeno Bay (500m from Astir Palace Hotel): high class restaurant serving French and international cuisine; pretty garden for *al fresco* dining; open 19.00–02.00 (tel: 91583).

Three Brothers, Kassiopi: describes its situation as 'next to the 300 year old plane tree'; Kassiopi's oldest *taverna* serves fresh seafood caught by the owner; reasonable prices and lots of character (tel: 81211).

THE NORTH-WEST

Delfini, Ag. Georgiou Bay: the first restaurant to be opened at this relatively new resort; freshly caught fish and lobster, also traditional Corfiot cooking; wonderful sunsets from its terrace above the beach; open 'till late' (tel: 0663-41378).

Bella Vista, Lakones: remarkable for its situation on a natural balcony commanding an incomparable view of Paleokastritsa and Liapades. The food is simple but well presented and reasonable.

Chez Georges the Rock, Paleokastritsa: large beachside restaurant specialising in fish, lobster and other seafood.

Odysseus, Odysseus Hotel, Paleokastritsa: hotel taverna specialising in Greek food at reasonable prices; spectacular sea view (tel: 0663-41209/22280/41342).

Top Sail Club, Glifada: has a good quality but expensive buffet alongside its ice cream parlour; delicious home-made cakes.

THE SOUTH

Mamma Lina, 18 Nafsikas St, Kanoni: friendly restaurant with tables set on a leafy terrace above the lagoon; large menu of Greek and Italian dishes; open 13.00–15.00 and 20.00–24.00 (tel: 22843).

Pierotto, Perama: reliable menu and panoramic views of Mouse Island and Chalikiopoulos Lagoon; steps go down to the causeway linking Perama with Kanoni.

Tripa, Kinopiastes: candlelit restaurant in old cottage with a patio at the rear; rustic atmosphere featuring baskets piled high with fruit and shelves of vintage wine festooned with cobwebs; genuine Corfiot cooking and exciting *mezethes*; live music and dancing. As Tripa is on the itinerary of coach trips, it is advisable to book (tel: 56333).

Spiros Taverna, Benitses: predominantly English food served overlooking the sea. This restaurant is part of a complex which includes a disco, video club and ice cream parlour; geared to the young.

Valentino, Moraitika (off the main road, opposite the pharmacy): menu includes Greek, Chinese and international food; tables on the terrace and in the garden; open 18.30–24.00.

Nightlife

DISCOTHEQUES

Most of the beach resorts offer at least one disco among their facilities, but the main concentration of nightspots is to be found in Mandouki and the northern outskirts of Corfu Town, Benitses, Kavos, Perama and the east coast strip from Gouvia to Pyrgi.

Discos include: **Mai Thai Disco**, Kanoni – English-owned, '60s night' on Sundays, open 21.00–03.00; **Adonis Disco**, Gouvia – central and popular, air-conditioned, free admission, open 22.00–03.00 (04.00 on Sats); **Breezee**, Dasia – largely British clientèle, free admission, open 22.30–03.00; **Babylon Disco**, Benitses – near the harbour, very popular, free admission, open 22.30–03.00; **Albatross Restaurant-Disco**, Ipsos – free admission, disco open

22.00–03.00; **Pink Panther Disco**, Pelekas – just outside the village, open 21.00–03.00; **Apocalypsis**, Mandouki (outskirts of Corfu Town) – fashionable and popular, admission 1000 dr., open 22.30–03.00; **La Boum**, Mandouki – in a converted stable block near the Apocalypsis with the same up-market image, admission charge and opening hours. Other discos include the **Bora-Bora**, **Coca Flash** and the **Hippodrome** in Mandouki; **Disco Bus Stop**, Ipsos; and the **Future**, Kavos.

GREEK DANCING, BOUZOUKI, ETC.

Many tavernas in Corfu Town and around the island have live entertainment of some description: **Corfu By Night**, for example, near the Tsavros junction north of Corfu Town is a large taverna/nightclub with cabaret and Greek dancing, and the **Tripa** taverna in Kinopiastes, offering traditional music and dancing plus as much food and wine as you can consume for 4000 dr., is a very popular evening venue, especially with organized excursions – **Taverna Gloupos**, in the nearby village of Milia, offers a similar night out (tel: 56283). *Bouzouki* music can be heard nightly at the popular **Esperides** night club in the Kerkyra Golf Hotel at Alikes Potamou. Most large hotels have a nightclub with dancing and a cabaret of some sort.

Organised displays of Greek folk dancing can also be seen regularly in the Old Fort, where the *Kerkyraikon Chorodrama* precedes the Sound and Light show at 21.00 every night (see below or tel: 30360, 39730 for more information), and at Danilia Village (see p.98).

Traditional dancing in the Old Fortress. Local Ionian dances include the communal *gastourikos* and the *agiriotikos*

SOUND AND LIGHT

From 15 May to the end of September a Sound and Light display is mounted daily in the Old Fort overlooking the Venetian harbour, the Mandraki. Commencing at 21.30, the commentary is in English on weekdays (Sir Laurence Olivier's is among the voices used) – except during August when the Monday shows are in Italian; at weekends the shows begin at 21.00 and are in Greek on Saturdays and French on Sundays. A display of Greek folk dancing precedes the Sound and Light (see above). An inclusive ticket for both shows cost 400 dr. in 1990 (students 180 dr.), or 300 dr. (150 dr.) for the Sound and Light only. Telephone 30520 or 30360 for further information.

CINEMAS

Cinemas usually show English, American or French films with Greek subtitles and are considerably cheaper than in the UK. In Corfu Town there are cinemas in G. Theotoki St (the Pallas) and Akadimias/Ger. Aspioti St (the Orfeus) and next to the Athletics Stadium in St. Padova St (the Oasis); there is also an open-air cinema, the Nausica, in Gr. Marasli St, which runs between San Rocco Sq. and Garitsa Bay one block west of Alexandras Ave.

CASINO

The casino on the upper floors of the Achilleion, one of only a handful in Greece, has recently been moved to the Hilton Hotel, Kanoni. It is only open to non-Greeks aged over 21; a passport is therefore required and men should wear jackets and ties. Entrance costs 950 dr. per night (4000 dr. per week), and roulette, blackjack, baccarat and chemin de fer are played. The minimum stake is 500 dr., maximum 250,000. The casino is open daily from 20.00–02.00 (03.00 on Saturdays).

PRACTICAL INFORMATION

Tourist Information

The Greek National Tourist Organization (NTOG) is in the west wing of the Palace of St Michael and St George, oppposite the Asian museum on Eleftherias Square, Corfu Town. It is open from 08.00–13.30 and 17.30–19.30 on weekdays, 09.00–12.00 on Saturdays (tel: 0661-30520/39730). The staff there speak reasonable English and are generally helpful, whilst the office itself is an excellent source of information, providing free maps, brochures and programmes in various languages. Unfortunately there are no NTOG branches elsewhere on the island, though many car hire offices, travel agents, etc., display tourist information notices: clearly such places are essentially commercially motivated but you may find answers to your queries in them.

Another possible source of information and advice, particularly if any problems arise, is the office of the Tourist Police, in the same building as the NTOG office but on the other side of the archway (open 07.00–22.00 daily, tel: 30265). They can also provide a list of rooms to let in private houses.

In Britain and Ireland, information about Corfu can be obtained from the Greek National Tourist Organisation, 4 Conduit, St, London W1R 0DJ (tel: 071-734-5997). In the USA, NTOG offices are at Olympic Tower, 645 Fifth Avenue, New York 10022 (tel: 421-5777), 168 North Michigan Avenue, Chicago, Ill. 60601 (tel: 782-1084) and 611 West 6th St, Suite 2198, Los Angeles, Calif. 90017 (tel: 626-6696).

Time

Greek time is, for most of the year, two hours ahead of the UK. As in the rest of Europe, however, summer time ends on the last weekend in September, so during October Corfu time is only one hour ahead.

Banks and Currency

Banks on Corfu are usually open from 08.00 to 14.00,

Monday to Thursday, and 08.00–13.00 on Fridays. Unlimited amounts of travellers' cheques can be exchanged at banks, though it is necessary to countersign the cheques in the presence of the cashier and to produce a passport as proof of identity. In addition post offices will change money; they may offer a better exchange rate and take less commission than the banks. There are also exchange bureaux in many of the resorts and most hotels and apartment complexes will exchange travellers' cheques or foreign currency at almost any time – some may charge more commission or offer a poorer rate of exchange than the banks, but this is by no means universally true.

For the tourist the wide variety of establishments willing to change foreign money is fortunate, as there are no banks outside Corfu Town. There they tend to congregate around San Rocco Square (Plateia Georgiou Theotoki), Kapodistriou St or Evg. Voulgareos St, where both the National Bank of Greece and the Commercial Bank can be found.

The currency is of course the Greek drachma: coins circulate in 1, 2 (two different designs), 5, 10, 20 and 50 (two designs, one silver, one bronze) drachma values, while there are notes for 50 (though it is being phased out), 100, 1000 and 5,000 drachmas.

Most major credit cards are widely accepted on Corfu, not only in restaurants but in larger supermarkets as well; Eurocheques (which can be cashed up to a value of 25,000 dr.) can also be used, but are not widely recognised outside Corfu Town itself.

Public Holidays

In addition to the movable feasts of 'Clean Monday' (*Kathari Deftera*, the first day of Orthodox Lent), Good Friday, Easter Day and Whit Monday, Corfu has public holidays on

1 January	New Year's Day (*Protochronia*)
6 January	Epiphany (*ton Theofanion*)
25 March	Independence Day
1 May	Labour Day
21 May	Ionian Day (the anniversary of the islands' union with Greece in 1864)
15 August	Assumption Day
28 October	'*Ochi*' Day ('No' Day, commemorating the Greeks' defiance of the Italian ultimatum to join the Axis Forces in World War Two, which precipitated their 1940 invasion)

| 25 December | Christmas Day |
| 26 December | St Stephen's Day |

Other local Saints' days and festivals are described on p.86–9.

Post

At the time of writing the cost of postage for ordinary letters and postcards to elsewhere in Europe was 80 dr. and to the USA, 100 dr.; postage within Greece begins at 30 dr. and by express delivery 220 dr. The service is not particularly swift: A holiday postcard may take up to four weeks to reach its destination. It is possible to buy stamps (*grammatosimi*) at many of the shops which sell postcards, also at some street kiosks or at tobacconists, both of which remain open at weekends.

The main post office (*tachydromio*) in Corfu Town is in Alexandras Avenue (two blocks south of San Rocco Square). It is open from 07.30 to 20.00 Mon–Fri (07.30–14.00 Sat, 07.30–13.00 Sun) for letters, parcels, stamp sales, *poste restante*, handling money orders and currency exchange. In the provinces there are branch post offices at Kastellani, Karoussades, Skripero and Lefkimmi and some of the larger resorts – for example Kassiopi and Paleokastritsa – have mobile post offices housed in a caravan which is parked in a prominent position during the season. Post boxes on Corfu are yellow.

Poste Restante should be addressed to *Poste Restante*, Corfu, Greece, and picked up at the main (Alexandras Avenue) post office; a passport will be necessary for identification.

Telephone

Telegrams and telephone calls are not handled by post offices, but are the province of the Greek Telecommunications Organization (OTE), whose main office in Corfu Town is at 3 Mantzarou Street (open 06.00 to midnight). Telegrams may be sent from here and local international telephone calls made, either by direct dialling or via the operator: for calls made here you queue for a numbered booth, paying the cashier after you have finished. In addition international calls may be dialled from all orange call-boxes (the blue kiosks are for local calls only): they accept all drachma coins but the smallest.

To dial abroad, it is necessary first to dial the country code (0044 for the UK, 001 for the USA, 00353 for Ireland), then the area code minus the first zero and finally the number you are calling. International calls are charged on a minimum of 3 minutes, and there is no off-peak rate – as an example the minimum 3-minute rate for calls to the UK was 442.5 dr. in 1990. Unfortunately international trunk lines often become busy in the tourist season and delays of up to an hour or more may be experienced before you can get through. A reverse-charge call may be made by dialling the international operator (151 for domestic, 161 for overseas calls), available 24 hours Mon-Fri. There is a second OTE office at 78 Kapodistriou St (behind the northern end of the Liston), open daily from 08.00–22.00.

When making local calls note that while the code for Corfu Town and the central part of the island is 0661, northern areas (for example Sidari, Kassiopi, Nissaki and Paleokastritsa) have the code 0663, and places south of Messongi 0662.

Health and Medical Care

Medical facilities in Corfu have received a bad press in past years, but standards are improving. The Agia Irini general hospital in Corfu Town is situated in Ioulias Andreadi St, west of San Rocco Square (the road to Paleokastritsa); it operates a 24-hour casualty department (tels: 30562 and 30033, emergencies/ambulance 39403).

Since Greece became a member of the European Community nationals of other EEC states are entitled to free medical treatment: to qualify, however, it is necessary to obtain a form E 111 from the DHSS (or equivalent) before leaving home. Any of Corfu's provincial clinics, such as those at Agios Mattheos (tel: 95310) and Kastellani (tel: 36945), can deal with minor ailments and again, on production of an E 111 form, treatment is free for EEC citizens.

First aid can be obtained at the First Aid Centre in Skaramanga Square, behind the Commercial Bank in Evg. Voulgareos St (tel: 39615 or phone 166 in emergency).

There is a large private clinic located in the Kaputsinos area on the outskirts of Corfu Town at 1 Ethniki Paleokas-trista (tel: 36044): dental facilities are also available here. Other (private) dental surgeries can be contacted on 34884, 37890 and 43855. Since dental treatment is not usually reclaimable from holiday health insurance, however, it is preferable to postpone treatment, if at all possible, until you are back home.

Pharmacies (*farmakia*) are quite widespread and usually open from 08.30–13.30 daily and 17.15–20.30 on Tuesdays,

The panorama from the 'Bella Vista' café

Boats in Kouloura harbour

(left) Twin beaches on Cape Arilla   (right) Peroulades
beach   (below) Paleokastritsa in spring

Thursdays and Fridays. They are recognisable by the sign of a red cross on a white background displayed outside. At least one *farmakion* stays open all night and on Sundays in Corfu Town – this is arranged on a rota system, and every pharmacy should display the address of the one that is open (in Greek). *Corfu News*, if you can obtain one, also lists them in English on a monthly basis. If in doubt, the police or passers-by will usually be able to direct you to the *farmakion* that is open. Sleeping pills, many stomach medications and artificial sweeteners are among the quite large number of drugs that are only available on prescription, but most chemists can give you useful health advice and administer first aid.

SUNSTROKE

The sun on Corfu is extremely hot throughout the summer and it is possible to get sunburnt even on cloudy days. Symptoms of sunstroke are headaches, rapid heartbeat, nausea, cramps and excessive tiredness. Take care, therefore, to obey the usual rules about increasing your exposure to the sun gradually, particularly between 11.00 and 15.00, and keep infants out of direct sunlight as far as possible. Protect the ears, nose, lips and back of the neck with sunscreen creams even when walking or driving around the island. Wide-brimmed hats and clothes with sleeves that can be rolled down are also a good idea. Sunstroke is exacerbated by the consumption of alcohol.

SNAKE-BITES

Few of the snakes on Corfu are poisonous; if bitten by a viper, however, do not cut the wound but apply a tourniquet above it and seek immediate medical help. The victim of a snake-bite should always be carried, not allowed to walk, thus spreading the poison through the body.

Tipping

Tipping is not a big issue on Corfu, since service charges have to be included in all hotel and restaurant bills. A small additional tip is however, always appreciated; a maximum of 10 per cent is generous for waiters, hairdressers and taxi-drivers when service has been expecially good.

Electricity

The voltage on Corfu is 220 volts; two-pin plugs are most

commonly used, so British visitors will do well to take an appropriate adaptor for hair-dryers, etc. Power is supplied from the mainland and cuts are nowadays rare.

Water

Corfu's tap water is perfectly safe to drink, but has a high mineral content that some may find upsetting. As elsewhere in Greece, bottled mineral water, most commonly of the still variety, is widely available and inexpensive – Loutraki, from the Athens area, is the most common. Corfu's locally famous Kardaki spring water is recommended, if you can find it.

Corfu's high winter rainfall and underground wells have traditionally made for plentiful water supplies, but with the growth of tourism and a series of dry winters this abundance is under threat, so water should not be wasted.

Lavatories

Public conveniences are rare. In Corfu Town there are lavatories at the north-western corner of San Rocco Square, the western end of the Old Port and near the entrance to the Old Fort on the Esplanade: also at the lidos by St Nicholas Gate and at Mon Repos – the last two make a small admission charge.

It is, however, perfectly acceptable to use the facilities in bars and restaurants. These are usually clean but almost always unlockable – perhaps a portable 'No Entry' sign might be a useful travel accessory! They also tend to lack toilet paper, perhaps as a deterrent to its disposal in the lavatory pan: the outflow pipe of a Greek lavatory is extremely narrow, so a bin is usually provided for used paper. There is usually a washbasin but not always an adjacent towel. Be prepared!

Radio and Newspapers

Greek national radio broadcasts the news in English on Monday and Thursday evenings at 18.00 on 100 megahertz FM. On Corfu in addition the ERT1 radio station (1008 kHz or 91.80 mHz) puts out a daily forecast of weather and sea conditions at 06.30 in English, and a news bulletin in English, French and German at 07.40 every day. In addition ERT2 (981 kHz) broadcasts news in English and French twice a day, at 14.20 and 21.20.

The World Service of the BBC can be received on various short-wave bands at different times of day, e.g. 1323 kHz, 226.76 metres.

British and other European newspapers are widely available at kiosks and news stands in Corfu Town and the major resorts, usually one day late. There are also a number of English-language magazines and newspapers published on the island, in particular the monthly (April–October) *Corfu News* (tel: 41071) available free from the Greek National Tourist Office and most travel agencies. In addition to useful tourist information it contains features on island life and characters, history, excursions and much else of interest.

Police

There are several distinct police forces in Greece. Of most use to visitors are the Tourist Police (pale grey uniform), a Greek invention: they are there to help visitors with accommodation, information and complaints – many of them speak foreign languages and wear flag badges indicating the fact. The Tourist Police are based in the west wing of the Palace of St Michael and St George close to the Tourist Information Office (tel: 30265). Unfortunately for tourists, in recent years there have been moves to subsume them within the Municipal Police, who fulfil a more traditional policing role. They drive white patrol cars and are based in Alexandras Ave (tel: 38568). Outside Corfu Town, the Rural Police (white motorcycle helmets) are contactable on tel: 109. In addition there are the Town Traffic Police (tel: 22353) and the Rural Traffic Police (tel: 30669). Lastly, the Aliens Police, concerned with passports, immigration, work permits, etc., are based in another part of the Palace of St Michael and St George (tel: 39494).

Consulates

The British vice-consulate is at 11 Alexandras Avenue, Corfu Town (at the end furthest from San Rocco Square, near the waterfront at Garitsa Bay). It is open from 08.00–14.00 Mondays to Fridays (tel: 30055 and 37995). The consulate can issue emergency passports, give advice on the transfer of funds in cases of theft or loss and contact relatives in case of an emergency. It is *not* authorized to pay bills, nor to interfere in civil litigation or give legal advice.

Germany, France, the Netherlands and Norway also maintain vice-consulates in Corfu, and several other European countries have representation. Other nationalities, however, including citizens of Eire, Australia, Canada, New Zealand and the USA, have to seek assistance from their embassies in Athens.

Religious Services

The national church is the Greek Orthodox. Anglican church services are held at Holy Trinity church, 21 Mavili St near the Ionian Parliament building (tel: 31467), which has services in English at 10.30 on Sunday mornings and Family Communion at 19.00 on the last Sunday of each month. The Roman Catholic Cathedral of St James, situated in the Town Hall Square, celebrates mass on Sundays at 07.30, 08.30 and 10.00, and on weekdays at 8.00 (except Saturdays, when Vespers is at 19.00). Services are held in English, German, French and Italian. Orthodox Sunday services are held between 07.00 and 10.30 at many churches, e.g. St Spiridon's and the Cathedral. There are no pews and worshippers can enter and leave as they wish. Corfu's only synagogue is located on Velissariou St, near the New Fort.

Emergency Telephone Numbers

Municipal Police	100
Rural Police	109
Fire	199
Forest Fire	191
Coast Guard	32655
Ambulance	39403
First Aid	30562
Emergency Road Assistance (ELPA)	104
Lost Property	39294

Travel agency, Pelekas

GEOLOGY AND CLIMATE

Geology

The most northerly and, at 370 sq. km the second largest of the Ionian islands, Corfu lies at the entrance to the Adriatic, only 2½ km from Albania and 74 km from Apulia in Italy.

Around 20 million years ago Corfu and the whole Ionian archipelago was joined to the mountain ranges of Albania and northern Greece: some authorities believe a 'land bridge' stretched from Lefkimmi to Epirus. Today the seven principal islands and their satellites extend in a 'string' parallel to the mainland; their structure is of limestone rising from valleys of fertile clay. This is an area of geological instability, but, as yet, Corfu has remained undamaged by earthquakes whereas its sister islands of Lefkas, Cefalonia and Zakynthos have suffered badly.

The highest mountains are in the north-east of Corfu where a massif extends from the bay of Apraos on the north coast to Barbati on the Corfu channel. Mount Pantokrator, at 906m, is the summit and is reachable by a rough road. A further range of rugged but lower mountains lying west of the Troumpeta pass culminates in Mount Arakli (405m) above Lakones, and plunges dramatically into the sea at Paleokastritsa and the bay of Liapades where the water is extremely deep. The southern slopes of Arakli give way to the extensive plain of Ropa, once a malarial marsh bordering the Ropa river but now an area of fertile pasture and the site of Corfu's only golf course.

Agii Deka (576m) is the island's second highest peak and rises directly between Agios Gordis on the west coast and Benitses on the east, its wooded limestone flanks forming glorious backdrops to both resorts. South of this range, running north to south and extending to the east coast, is the Messonghi river basin, another wetland, partly reclaimed for agriculture. The extreme south of Corfu is fairly low-lying with shallow seas in the east and the salt water lagoon of Lake Korission behind a barrage of sand dunes in the west. The most southerly point, Cape Asprokavos, is a lofty limestone headland facing the island of Paxos.

Corfu Town sits on a high limestone promontory half way up the east coast and overlooks areas of marshland on either side: the shallow inlet of Chalikiopoulos, part of which has

Eroded rock formations near Sidari

been reclaimed to build the airport, lies to the south and the flat valley of the river Potamos extends north to Dasia. Fertile land borders the river; the coastal salt marshes are being drained for touristic development and the improvement of the main road north.

The extreme north of Corfu features lowish hills of clay and sand intersected by streams and areas of swamp which are potentially cultivable. The clay deposits can most interestingly be seen in the cliffs of Sidari and Peroulades where the strata are clearly visible: stacks and channels are still being carved out by the sea, notably the 'canal d'amour' at Sidari. Just east of Cape Agios Ekaterinis (Corfu's most northerly point) is the Andinioti lagoon, which, although very close to the sea at Agios Spiridon beach, has fresh water.

Climate

Corfu lies in the Ionian Sea at 39.5° North, its northern tip being on the same latitude as the southern shore of Apulia in Italy. The climate is Mediterranean with a hot dry summer, changeable spring and autumn followed by a mild wet winter with average temperatures of around 10°C. Relatively high humidity throughout the year accounts for the surprisingly green landscape which is untypical of Greek islands. The annual rainfall (about 100cm – comparable with parts of Derbyshire) is in fact higher here and extends for a longer period than anywhere else in Greece.

January and February are the coldest months. However, frost is rare and Mount Pantokrator has only an occasional dusting of snow whereas the ever visible mountains of neighbouring Albania and Epirus are white throughout the winter months. A chill wind from the north-east, blowing to Corfu from the Albanian mainland, is known locally as the *bora* but as the *gregos* elsewhere in Greece. The island is also subjected in winter to the slightly less cold *garbis* from the south-west and the damp southerly *ostria*.

Spring arrives very early and lasts until May when the onset of summer is heralded by the flickering of fireflies, temperatures above 20°C and a change of wind direction from the south-east (*sirokos*) to the westerly *ponentes*. By mid-June the weather is usually predictable, with long hours of sunshine, high temperatures, negligible rainfall and breezes from the north-west. Unlike the Aegean islands, which are fanned all summer from this quarter, Corfu is relatively calm. The north-west wind (*maestro*) can be gusty and tends to blow up during the afternoons, dying at sunset. Occasionally it can create storm conditions over periods as long as three to five days after which it suddenly ceases. Legend has it that Odysseus was washed ashore at Ermones (see p.64) having being tossed for two days and nights in heavy seas, after which 'a breathless calm set in'. This is certainly an apt description of a *maestro*. A similar storm assisted the Corfiots in vanquishing the Turks on 11 August 1716.

The island's humidity is fairly high and visibility is clearest when the cool *levandes* brings air from the east; the *sirokos* from North Africa renders the atmosphere hot and sticky with thick haze. The remaining wind is the *tramontana* from the true north which does not prevail but can occur at any time of the year.

The summer drought in Corfu is followed by spectacular thunderstorms during the second half of September, ushering in cooler and cloudier days in October. Depressions tracking eastward across the Mediterranean combine with the Adriatic's own areas of low pressure to create showery conditions. Winter is said to begin on St Philip's day (4 November) and December brings frequent heavy rain during which the streams turn into rushing torrents and the island's reservoirs are replenished.

Corfu's climate contributes hugely to its prosperity. The warm sun and reliable rainfall ensure a good growing season while the glorious summers attract the tourists who do not encounter the water shortages common to most Greek islands.

A weather forecast in English is broadcast daily by the local radio station in Corfu at 06.30 local time on 1008 khz (AM).

AVERAGE TEMPERATURES 1960–1990

	Average max. °C	Average min. °C	Sunshine hours	Rain mm.	Relative humidity	Sea temp. °C
Jan	13.9	5.3	139	153.0	74.8	15.5
Feb	14.2	5.7	139	139.9	74.2	15.1
Mar	15.9	6.8	159	107.0	73.0	14.4
April	19.0	9.1	210	63.7	72.5	15.6
May	23.8	12.7	312	38.3	69.1	18.9
June	28.0	16.2	348	11.6	62.9	21.4
July	30.9	18.1	396	7.3	59.0	23.8
Aug	31.2	18.5	360	16.9	61.3	24.3
Sept	27.7	16.4	273	84.5	69.5	22.7
Oct	23.2	13.2	202	152.3	74.2	22.5
Nov	18.8	9.7	128	193.4	77.1	18.5
Dec	15.5	6.7	101	185.2	76.5	17.0

Source: Hellenic National Meteorological Service, Station Kerkyra

NATURAL HISTORY

Flowering Plants

The richest floral displays are to be seen between March and the end of May but, from February onwards, the coastlines are alive with colour. Spring arrives slightly later in the inland areas and the sequence of flowering advances to the Pantokrator massif where, at altitudes of above 700m, the same species bloom up to a month later than at the coast. July and August, the hottest and driest months, are the least rewarding for botanists; however, two of Corfu's most spectacular flowers, the sea squill and the sea daffodil, both unmistakable, are flowering then. After the thunderstorms of late summer, a 'second spring' begins in September or October with the appearance of crocuses and cyclamens, followed by snowdrops in November.

The following list is not a full inventory of Corfiot flora but serves to show something of the wide variety of plants on the island and the most rewarding times to look for them. Keen botanists should carry with them *Flowers of Greece and the Aegean* by Anthony Huxley and William Taylor.

Acanthus balcanicus bear's breech (*Apouranos*). A tall substantial spike of whitish flowers veined with purple rises from a rosette of large deeply indented leaves whose outline was imitated in the Corinthian capitals of ancient Greek architecture. May – July.

Alcea pallida eastern hollyhock (*Agriomolocha*). Tall spikes of large pink flowers are seen on hillsides, especially near olive groves. May – July.

Alkanna tinctoria dyer's alkanet (*Vaforiza*). Bushy perennial with hairy leaves and stems and bright blue flowers; usually grows near the sea. The Greek name means 'dye-root', so called because the roots contain a red pigment. March – May.

Allium sphaerocephalum round-headed leek. One of a large family, this leek has pyramidal purple flowers on long stems. June – August.

Anacamptis pyramidalis pyramidal orchid. Tall orchid with dense cluster of deep pink flowers; waste ground. March – July.

Anagallis arvensis pimpernel (*Anagallis*). The familiar scarlet pimpernel is found alongside its cobalt blue counterpart on dry ground. March – Sept.

Anemone blanda (Anemona tou vounou). Blue 'daisy' with whorls of triple leaves lower down the stem. A low-growing plant found in woods or high scrubland. March – June.

Anemone coronaria crown anemone (*Anemona*). A pink, purple or red anemone growing in stony places or in scrubland. The flower is up to 5cm. in diameter. Feb – April.

Anthemis chia Greek chamomile (*Agria margarita*). Aromatic plant with white 'daisy' flowers and bright green fleshy leaves which can be dried and made into chamomile tea. March – May.

Antirrhinum majus tortuosum snapdragon (*Skylaki*). The wild form of the familiar garden flower: can be pink or yellow. The Greek name means 'small dog', so called because the flower resembles the lips of an animal. March – May.

Arisarum vulgare friar's cowl (*Lychnaraki*). Stripy purple spathe (sheath), imitating a cowl, issues from arrow-shaped shiny leaves. Nov – March.

Asphodelus albus white asphodel (*Asfodili*). Tall rush-like plant with spike of white flowers striped with brown; grows on stony hillsides. April – August.

Aubrieta deltoidea aubretia. Familiar to gardeners, this rock plant has greyish leaves shaped like the Greek letter 'delta', hence its name. April – June.

Calystegia soldanella sea bindweed (*Periplokadi*). Pale pink flower with white stripes and kidney-shaped leaves. May – Sept.

Campanula ramosissima campanula (*Kampanoula*). Wide-open bellflowers of deepest blue: the plant can take the form of a small bush. April – May.

Campanula spathulata campanula (*Kampanoula*). Delicate mauve bells are borne erect on weak stems. Stony places. May – Sept.

Campanula versicolor campanula (*Kampanoula*). Found only in northern Greece and Corfu, these beautiful flowers are deep blue in the centre and paler at the edge. Shady places. May – Sept.

Centaurea cyanus cornflower (*Anthos*). More familiar in Britain in florists' shops, this handsome dark blue flower grows on arable land. May – August.

Centranthus ruber valerian (*Analatos*). Clusters of red or pink flowers are borne on long stalks; the whole plant clings to cliffs, rocks or walls. April – August.

Chrysanthemum coronarium crown daisy (*Mantilida*). Handsome tall yellow or yellow and white daisy growing by roadsides or on waste ground. March – June.

Chrysanthemum segetum corn marigold (*Agriomantilida*). Tall yellow daisy growing on cultivated ground where it can be a troublesome weed. April – August.

Colchicum autumnale meadow saffron (*Volchiko*). The pale mauve autumn crocus is beautiful but poisonous and grows in damp meadows. August – Sept.

Convallaria majalis lily of the valley (*Peka*). Needing no description, this fragrant flower favours damp cool areas. April – June.

Convolvulus althaeoides mallow-leaved bindweed (*Agrio periplokadi*). A trailer and a climber; the pretty pink flowers, 4cm. across, open in sunlight. April – August.

Campanula spathulata, May

Crepis rubra pink hawksbeard (*Starida*). A pale pink 'double daisy' with toothed leaves; grows in olive groves and stony ground. April – June.

Crocus cancellatus (*Kastanea*). The Greek name for this pale violet or white crocus derives from the corms being edible when roasted like chestnuts. Rocky hillsides. Sept – Nov.

Crocus olivierii (*Krokos*). Spectacular orange flowers on low-growing plant found on bare stony slopes. Feb – April.

Cyclamen graecum cyclamen (*Kyklamino*). Miniature cyclamen whose flowers vary from pink to crimson; found on stony ground and heathland. The large heart-shaped leaves appear after the flowers have gone. Sept – Dec.

Cymbalaria muralis ivy-leaved toadflax (*Perouka*). A climber of neat habit, having small mauve flowers reminiscent of the garden linaria and leaves like ivy; shady walls. May – August.

Cytinus ruber   red cytinus (*Lykos tou ladanou*). Parasitic plant which favours the pink cistus as its host. White fleshy flowers issue from red fleshy scales. May – June.

Delphinium peregrinum   violet larkspur (*Delfinion*). Bluish-purple blooms as in the similar garden plant; waste ground, notably by the road up to the monastery at Paleokastritsa. May – June.

Dianthus carthusianorum   Carthusian pink (*Garifalia*). Small bright pink flowers are borne in clusters on tall slender stems; leaves are narrow. Grows in woodland at high altitudes and is one of the large family of *dianthus* which means, in Greek, 'flower of Zeus'. June – Sept.

Ecballium elaterium   squirting cucumber (*Pikrangouria*). Grows on waste land and has gherkin-like fruits which explode when touched, expelling the seed and a poisonous liquid. Apr – Sept.

Echium plantagineum   purple viper's bugloss (*Vouglosson*). This variety has larger flowers than the common viper's bugloss but enjoys similar habitats: waste land, roadsides and sandy areas. April – July.

Epilobium angustifolium   rosebay willowherb. Frequently seen in western Europe on river banks and railway embankments, these tall pink 'spires' grow in damp places and in woodland. June – Sept.

Eryngium maritimum   sea holly (*Galanochorto*). Bluish-green plant with globular azure flowers which are also prickly; sand dunes and beaches. May – August.

Ferula communis   giant fennel (*Narthikas*). Can be 3m. tall with umbels of up to 0.5m. across, florets are yellow. Traditionally the flower in which Prometheus brought fire from heaven. March – June.

Fritillaria graeca   fritillary. Striped brown and green inverted 'tulip' which invariably nods in the breeze; bare rocky places. March – May.

Galanthus nivalis reginae olgae   snowdrop (*Skoularikia*). The leaves appear after the flowers; woods or stony pastures. Oct – Dec.

Gladiolus segetum   field gladiolus (*Spathochorto*). Bright pink flowers; gladioli grow in profusion on arable land. May – June.

Glaucium flavum   yellow horned poppy (*Gialopikro*). Golden flowers and glaucous grey leaves; grows on shingle and sand. April – July.

Helianthemum nummularium   rockrose. Creeping woody plant with, usually, yellow flowers; resembles a miniature cistus. Open, stony places. March – June.

Hypericum apollinis   St. John's wort (*Agouthanos*). Greek version of the familiar St. John's wort; prefers rocky places in full sun. April – June.

Iris florentina   common iris (*Aspros krinos*). Tall stalks of white flowers tinged with purple. The rhizome is used in perfume production.

Iris sisyrinchium Barbary nut (*Afti tou lagou*). The corm has a nutty flavour! Bright blue flowers with white and yellow markings; prefers dry places near the sea. March – May.

Leucanthemum vulgare marguerite (*Margarita*). A white daisy with serrated leaves; fields and hillsides. May – June.

Limonium sinuatum statice. Also known as 'winged sea lavender', the bluish-purple papery flowers growing from compact rosettes are well known as 'everlasting' and used in pot-pourri. Flowers all summer on the shore, particularly in the north-west.

Linum perenne perennial flax (*Linari*). A meadow plant, having delicate pale blue flowers on tall, rather insubstantial stems. April – May.

Lupinus micranthus lupin (*Loupinari*). Dark blue lupin up to 40cm. tall; grows in olive groves and waste ground. Feb – April.

Malva sylvestris common mallow (*Molocha*). Grows to heights of more than a metre and bears pink or purple flowers. March – May.

Matthiola sinuata sea stock (*Agriovioletta*). Pink or purple fragrant flowers and greyish leaves. March – May.

Medicago marina sea medick. A prostrate plant found on beaches; woolly leaves and clusters of yellow flowers. March – May.

Melittis melissophyllum bastard balm. Found on wooded high ground, this aromatic plant has nettle-like leaves and bright pink, white and purple flowers. May – July.

Mesembryanthemum crystallinum ice plant (*Vouzi*). Creeping succulent growing on coastal rocks; the large cream flowers bloom among 'frosted' leaves. April – June.

Minuartia stellata. Low-growing mossy 'cushion' with single white five-petalled flowers, found on rocks in the mountains. July – August.

Muscari commutatum dark grape hyacinth (*Volvos*). Reminiscent of the garden grape hyacinth; grows on cliffs and hillsides. March – April.

Muscari comosum tassel hyacinth (*Askordoulakas*). A very tall grape hyacinth bearing two groups of flowers on one stalk; fields and waste land. March – May.

Narcissus poeticus hellenicus pheasant's eye (*Zamvaki*). Sweet-scented flower familiar to gardeners; the plant is narcotic and is also associated with the legend of Echo and Narcissus. May – June.

Narcissus serotinus autumn narcissus (*Manoussaki*). Small fragrant white flower with gold centre and tallish stem; usually grows near the sea. Sept – Dec.

Nigella damascena love-in-a-mist. This well-known garden plant grows wild in olive groves and by the roadside. March – May.

Onosma frutescens golden drop (*Xylothroumbos*). Bushy perennial having bristly stems and leaves and pendulous flowers of pale yellow edged with red; woods and scrubland. April – May.

Ophrys fusca brown bee orchid (*Melissaki*). Velvety blue and brown flower with distinctive blue spot. Feb – May.

Ophrys tenthredinifera sawfly orchid (*Kori*). Very pretty pink and gold oval flowers with green veins. Feb – May.

Orchis italica (*Salepi*). The pale pink flowers imitate the human shape and are borne in loose round clusters. The tuber yields a powder from which a soothing drink, *salepi*, is made. April – May.

Orchis laxiflora loose-flowered orchid (*Salepi*). Very tall orchid (up to 1m.) with spike of up to twenty crimson flowers. Until relatively recently in Corfu, the tubers were made into 'bulb tea'. March – June.

Orlaya grandiflora. A distinctive flat cluster of white flowers, the outermost florets being many times larger than the inner ones; roadsides and other dry places. June – July.

Ornithogalum nanum star of Bethlehem. A dwarf of the species, the six-petalled starlike flowers grow on short stalks out of bare rough ground. April – May.

Pancratium maritimum sea daffodil (*Krinos tis thalassas*). Fragrant papery white flower resembling a daffodil; sand dunes and beaches. July – Sept.

Papaver rhoeas corn poppy (*Paparouna*). The brilliant scarlet poppy is widespread in fields and on waste land throughout the island. April – June.

Parnassia palustris grass of Parnassus. White flowers with conspicuous veins and five petals are borne on stalks up to 30cm. high; damp meadows or waste land. July – Sept.

Primula veris cowslip (*Dacraki*). The well known cowslip may be found in woodland areas, particularly in the mountains. April – May.

Saponaria calabrica soapwort (*Sapounochorto*). Clusters of pale pink flowers are borne on stems up to 40cm. which issue from a creeping rhizome; rocky places. An ancient remedy for stomach problems and rheumatism. June – Sept.

Saxifraga scardica saxifrage (*Empetron*). Delicate five-petalled white or pink flowers grow from rosettes of stiff greyish leaves; rocky places in the mountains. June – August.

Scabiosa atropurpurea sweet scabious. Flat heads of purple to misty blue florets on long stalks; dry places or meadows. May – July.

Silene colorata catchfly (*Fouskies*). Tiny pink flowers on a cushion of minute leaves; abundant on sand and rocks. March – April.

Sternbergia lutea sternbergia (*Krinaki*). Resembles a yellow crocus; grows on sunny hillsides or in fields. Sept – Oct.

Tragopogon porrifolius salsify (*Lagochorto*). Grows up to 75cm. with flowers like a purple dandelion and narrow leaves; dry areas. March – May.

Trifolium purpureum purple clover (*Trifylli*). Pinkish-purple flowers on long stems distinguish this clover from related species; sunny meadows. March – July.

Tussilago farfara coltsfoot (*Chamoleuka*). A familiar wild flower in Britain, this compact yellow 'daisy' has leaves believed to act as a remedy for coughs and asthma. Feb – May.

Mulleins on Angelokastro, Mt Arakli in the background

Urginea maritima sea squill (*Skylokremida*). A tall spike of white flowers bursts from an enormous bulb. Dry, stony places. Aug – Oct.

Verbascum speciosum mullein (*Flomos*). Very tall spire of yellow flowers, the whole plant sometimes reaching 2m. in height. Impressive display adorns Angelokastro. May – August.

Vinca major greater periwinkle (*Agriolitsa*). Familiar prostrate creeper with large blue flowers found in woods and by streams. March – June.

Trees and Shrubs

Corfu is justly renowned for being the greenest of all the Greek islands: its hot dry summers and mild wet winters ensure that all forms of plant life flourish.

The predominant trees are olive and cypress which together blanket the hills and valleys. In addition to the endemic trees and shrubs, some of which are catalogued below, many others have been introduced to the island and are now naturalised in their Mediterranean environment. These include the eucalyptus, Indian bead tree (*Melia azedarach*), jacaranda and the Peruvian pepper tree (*Schinus molle*). Fruit trees are an important feature near the villages: almonds, apricots, lemons, oranges, cherries, apples and pears all grow well.

Good descriptions of the island's trees and shrubs are found in *Trees and Bushes of Britain and Europe* by Oleg Polunin; many are also described by Anthony Huxley and William Taylor in their *Flowers of Greece and the Aegean*.

Ailanthus altissima tree of heaven. A true native of Corfu, as at

Old Perithia; large leaves, yellow flowers followed by reddish fruits. July – August.

Arbutus unedo   strawberry tree (*Koumaria*). The edible red fruit (in Greek 'koumara') resembles a strawberry whereas the flowers are like pink or cream lilies-of-the-valley. Sept – Nov.

Capparis spinosa   caper (*Kappari*). Eyecatching wall plant having large white flowers with mauve stamens; the capers are the pickled flower buds. June – Sept.

Cercis siliquastrum   Judas tree (*Koutsoukia*). Although wild, it has been much planted in Corfu Town. The vivid pink flowers sprout from the bare wood and are followed by roundish leaves. Traditionally the tree from which Judas Iscariot hanged himself. March – April.

Cistus incanus creticus   pink cistus (*Ladania*). Quite common on Corfu, this aromatic shrub has showy pink flowers, each lasting one day. March – June.

Cistus salvifolius   sage-leaved cistus (*Kounoukla*). Often grows near the pink cistus; has large white flowers and is not aromatic. March – May.

Coronilla emerus   scorpion senna. Shrub with clusters of bright yellow flowers which later form long pods. March – May.

Cupressus sempervirens   cypress (*Kyparissi*). Columnar tree with small greyish cones; a feature of countless Corfiot hillsides.

Erica verticillata   heather (*Chamoriki*). A bushy heath with pink bell-shaped flowers; rocky and sandy terrain.

Euphorbia dendroides   tree spurge (*Galastivi*). Can grow up to 2m. high and usually in a perfect hemisphere; flowers greenish yellow and stems red. Coastal hills: viz. Paleokastritsa. March – June.

Ficus carica   fig (*Fikos*). Can grow to 5m.; fruit very distinctive, turning from green to purple as it ripens. June – July.

Jasminum fruticans   shrubby jasmine (*Yasemi*). Semi-evergreen shrub with scentless yellow flowers; similar to the garden climber. April – June.

Laurus nobilis   sweet bay (*Dafni*). Evergreen aromatic tree whose smooth green leaves are used in cooking; small cream flowers are followed by black berries.

Lavandula stoechas   French lavender (*Agriolevanda*). Familiar to all, and used in perfume, this shrub is wholly aromatic. Feb – June.

Lavatera arborea   tree mallow. Very tall mallow with many branches; pinkish-purple flowers; coastal areas. April – Sept.

Ligustrum vulgare   privet (*Agriomyrtia*). Much used in the UK as a hedging shrub, the privet grows wild in Greece; white flowers. May – July.

Lonicera etrusca   honeysuckle (*Agrio-agioklima*). A non-fragrant honeysuckle with whitish-yellow flowers which are pink in the bud. The ancient Greeks used honeysuckle motifs in their decoration. May – June.

Myrtis communis   myrtle (*Myrtia*). Much associated with classical Greece, where it symbolised peace and honour, every part of this shrub is aromatic. Dark green leaves and white flowers are followed by black berries; gives its name to Myrtiotissa. May – July.

Nerium oleander oleander (*Pikrodafni*). Most noticeable when it is in bloom: striking pink flowers sprout from grey-green foliage; favours stony places. May – July.

Olea europaea olive (*Elia*). This grey-green tree with twisted boughs is an integral part of the Corfiot scene and lives to an immense age: those at Messongi are thought to be 700 years old.

Oreganum vulgare oregano (*Rigani*). Also known as marjoram, this herb has pink flowers and small aromatic leaves which are an important ingredient in Corfiot cooking. July – Sept.

Paliurus spina-christi Christ's thorn (*Paliouri*). Large spiny shrub of the blackthorn family; light green glossy leaves and clusters of small starry yellow flowers.

Phlomis fruticosa Jerusalem sage (*Afaka*). Beloved of bees, this shrub with whorls of golden flowers and large soft leaves is prolific on dry hillsides. March – June.

Pinus halepensis Aleppo pine (*Pevko*). Lofty tree with bright green needles; tapped for its resin which is used for making *retsina*.

Pistacia lentiscus mastic tree (*Skinos*). The leathery leaves emanate a resinous scent; reddish-brown flowers followed by small black berries. As well as having curative properties, the resin is used as a kind of chewing gum. March – May.

Punica granatum pomegranate (*Rodia*). Smallish tree with attractive scarlet flowers followed by pomegranates in the autumn. Both flowers and fruit produce a red dye and the fruit was deemed by the ancient Greeks to symbolise fertility. May – July.

Quercus coccifera Kermes oak (*Prinari*). Also known as the holly oak, this small tree has prickly leaves and bears acorns. It is host to the scale insect which produces a red dye.

Quercus ilex holm oak (*Aria*). Growing on hillsides, this tall evergreen bears pointed acorns and yields very hard wood.

Rhamnus alaternus buckthorn (*Kitrinoxylo*). Widespread throughout the Mediterranean, it is most recognisable in summer when it bears glossy red, purple and black berries. Small yellow flowers. March – April.

Rosa sempervirens wild rose (*Agriotriantafylia*). An evergreen rambler with white flowers in clusters; seen in hedges or climbing cypress trees. Feb – July.

Smilax aspera sarsaparilla (*Arkoudovatos*). Rambling evergreen with thorns; often trails in tangles on the ground; red berries. Sept – Nov.

Spartium junceum Spanish broom (*Sparto*). Occurring on hillsides all over Corfu, this unmistakable shrub is a blaze of golden sweetly scented flowers in spring and early summer. May – July.

Styrax officinalis storax (*Stouraki*). The bark of this deciduous shrub or small tree produces a gum used in making incense. The leaves are shiny green with woolly grey undersides; the clustered flowers white and bell-shaped. April – May.

Tamarix dalmatica tamarisk (*Armiriki*). Small tree with feathery foliage, dark brown bark and racemes of white flowers; found near coasts. Spring – summer.

Vitex agnus-castus   chaste tree (*Alygaria*). Deciduous shrub or tree bearing spikes of mauve flowers reminiscent of buddleia. Once believed to have powers to preserve chastity, the tree was sacred to the goddess Hera. June – Sept.

Birds

Corfu's mild climate and wide range of habitats contribute to the island's reputation as an ideal birdwatching environment. It is inhabited and visited by a large proportion of the species seen in western Europe; additionally the amateur ornithologist will be rewarded by sightings of birds which confine themselves to the eastern Mediterranean. Moreover, the spring and autumn bring opportunities to spot passage migrants on their way to and from Egypt and Libya. In winter the lagoons host flocks of teal and wigeon, many of which fall foul of the 'sportsman's' gun.

The precipitous cliffs of the north-west attract hundreds of sea birds while the predators haunt the mountains. For overall variety the lakes of Andinioti in the north and Korission in the south are highly recommended. Not only do these venues harbour water fowl, but their sandy and reedy perimeters provide perfect conditions for countless other birds. Waders and marsh-loving species also occur in the Ropa valley and on the Lefkimmi salt flats. Corfu Town is the place for swallows, swifts and martins and the extensive olive groves shelter many of the shyer birds.

Among the more colourful specimens are the bee-eater, roller, golden oriole, hoopoe and kingfisher. The kingfisher is to be spotted flying low and straight over the sea as well as fishing by inland waters.

Several owls inhabit the island: most notably Corfiot is the Scops owl, which can be heard calling plaintively on most nights. It is dubbed the 'Gionis' owl and its cry is popularly interpreted as 'Yianni! Yianni!' like the anguished call of a girl to her missing lover.

The list of birds below is intended only as an outline to show their immense variety; anyone interested in identification should carry a copy of Heinzel, Fitter and Parslow, *The Birds of Britain and Europe with North Africa and the Middle East.*

Avocet   *Recurvirostra avosetta* (*Avoketa*). Distinctive tall black and white wader with long legs and upturned bill; around the lagoons or on Lefkimmi salt flats.

Barn owl   *Tyto alba* (*Peplokoukouvagia*). The white faced barn owl with its eerie screech is not particularly common; nests in caves.

Bee-eater   *Merops apiaster (Melissophagos)*. Brightly coloured bird: its crown and back are chestnut, underparts jade green and throat bright yellow; seen in open country and in the sand dunes beside Lake Korission.

Blackbird   *Turdus merula (Kossyfos)*. A bird needing no introduction, it prefers forested areas or orchards.

Blackcap   *Sylvia atricapilla (Mavroskoufis)*. As its name suggests, this warbler is easy to identify; frequents woodland or scrub; high-pitched melodious song.

Black-headed bunting   *Emberiza melanocephala (Krasopouli)*. Smallish but showy yellow-breasted bird with a black head; seen in olive groves and in the 'maquis'; warbles like a canary.

Black redstart   *Phoenicurus ochruros (Karavouniaris)*. Fairly common on Corfu, this bird is 14cm. long, black and white with a russet tail.

Blue rock thrush   *Monticola solitarius (Galazokotsufas)*. Handsome dark blue bird, 20cm. long, seen in rocky areas and on buildings.

Blue tit   *Parus caeruleus*. Tiny blue and yellow bird familiar in British gardens; seen here in orchards, gardens and olive groves.

Bullfinch   *Pyrrhula pyrrhula (Kokkinolaimis)*. Unmistakable large finch with rose-pink breast and black head; resident in Corfiot orchards.

Buzzard   *Buteo buteo (Megas)*. Large bird of prey, mid or light brown with a barred tail; its call is gull-like.

Cetti's warbler   *Cettia cetti (Psevaidoni)*. Extremely shy small brown bird which sings a loud staccato song.

Chaffinch   *Fringilla coelebs (Spinos)*. The commonest finch in Europe confines itself to the higher woods in summer.

Chiffchaff   *Phylloscopus collybita*. The English name imitates this warbler's call; its plumage is greyish-brown tinged with yellow.

Cirl bunting   *Emberiza cirlus (Sirlotsichlono)*. Resembles the yellowhammer but has a grey crown and black throat; feeds on seeds in arable land.

Collared dove   *Streptopelia decaocto (Dekochtoura)*. Originating in western Asia, this species is now resident in most of western Europe; its pinkish-beige plumage and trisyllabic 'coo' are familiar in Britain.

Common sandpiper   *Tringa hypoleucos*. Small grey-brown and white wader preferring small pools to large lakes; winter visitor.

Crested lark   *Galerida cristata (Katsoulieris)*. A native of northern Greece, this small brown and white flecked bird has a paler breast and a prominent crest; fairly common in and near villages.

Dalmatian pelican   *Pelicanus crispus (Argyropelekanos)*. Very large (up to 1.8m) and recognisable bird with long pouched bill; lakes and the Chalikiopoulos lagoon.

Egyptian vulture   *Neophron percnopterus (Asproparis)*. White vulture with black wing tips and yellow head; summer visitor.

Golden eagle *Aquila chrysaetos (Chrysaetos).* Majestic soaring bird of prey; frequents the Pantokrator massif and the mountains above Ermones.

Golden oriole *Oriolus oriolus (Sykophagos).* Spectacular bright yellow bird with black wings which visits the island in spring and summer. More uncommon these days as uncontrolled shooting has diminished its numbers; olive groves in north and north-west of the island.

Goldfinch *Carduelis carduelis (Karderina).* A familiar sight on Corfu, this bright little bird is typically seen on thistles.

Goshawk *Accipiter gentilis (Diplosaino).* A handsome bird of prey with barred underparts and tail; resident in woods on Corfu, it feeds on small mammals, birds and reptiles.

Great spotted woodpecker *Dendrocopus major (Pardalotsiklitara).* Endemic to northern Greece, it can be seen in Corfu's woodland. Predominantly black and white, it has patches of brilliant red on its head and under its tail.

Great tit *Parus major (Kalogeros).* The largest of its family, it lives in wooded areas but is also seen in the towns in winter.

Greenfinch *Carduelis chloris (Floros).* One of the larger finches; eats insects on farmland and in olive groves.

Green woodpecker *Picus viridis (Prasinotsiklitara).* Beautiful green and yellow bird with red crown; resident in the woods. Its call is a laughing 'yaffle'.

Grey heron *Ardea cinerea (Stachtotsiknias).* Grey and white bird, tall and 'hunched'; is typically seen standing on one leg in areas of mud and shallow water.

Herring gull *Larus argentatus (Asimoglaros).* Commonest of the local gulls, it is also the biggest; bright yellow bill with a vermilion spot.

Hoopoe *Upupa epops (Tsalapeteinos).* Easy to identify and very handsome, this bird is cinnamon-coloured with black and white striped wings and similar erectile crest. A spring and summer visitor, its call: 'hoo hoo hoo' is also distinctive.

House martin *Delichon urbica (Spitochelidono).* 'Urban swallow' seen in great numbers wheeling over Corfu Town where it attaches its mud nests to buildings; summer visitor.

Kingfisher *Alcedo atthis (Alkyona).* Well known throughout Europe, this colourful bird frequents the lakes and coasts in winter; favours the Messonghi river.

Linnet *Carduelis cannabina (Kokkinospiza).* Attractive finch with a red breast; lives on seeds and prefers to haunt the 'maquis'.

Little owl *Athene noctua (Koukouvagia).* Sometimes seen during the day and heard 'imitating' a curlew; perches on posts on farmland, searching for rodents and small birds.

Little tern *Sterna albifrons (Nanoglaros).* A summer visitor to Corfu, this graceful grey and white sea bird has a black head and a yellow bill with black tip.

Magpie *Pica pica (Karakaxa).* As common in Greece as in the

UK, this large black and white bird has no preferred habitat and is omnivorous.

Mallard *Anas platyrhynchos (Prasinokefali papia)*. Familiar wild duck with dark green head and white collar; lakes and rivers.

Mediterranean gull *Larus melanocefalus (Skylokoutavos)*. A black-headed gull which lacks the black tail feathers of the eponymous bird

Moorhen *Gallinula chloropus (Agriornitha)*. Small black water fowl which swims with jerky head movements.

Nightingale *Luscinia megarhynchos (Aidoni)*. A summer visitor whose melodious voice is heard by night or day.

Nuthatch *Sitta europaea (Dendrotsopanakos)*. Resident in woodland, it finds insects in the fissures of tree trunks and supplements its diet with acorns and pine cones.

Oystercatcher *Haematopus ostralegus (Streidofagos)*. Black and white wader with long red beak and pink legs; characteristically seen on the seashore, digging for shellfish.

Peregrine falcon *Falco peregrinus (Petritis)*. A fairly common hawk: has a dark grey back and lighter mottled underside; the outline in flight resembles an anchor; preys on young birds.

Pochard *Aythya ferina (Kynigopapia)*. This duck is resident on the island and frequents the lakes and areas of brackish water; has a chestnut head, dark brown breast and light grey back.

Purple heron *Ardea purpurea (Porphyrotsiknais)*. Has a more snake-like neck than the familiar grey heron and is darker in colour; habitat similar but it is a shy summer visitor.

Raven *Corvus corax (Korax)*. Large (65cm) totally black bird usually seen on very high cliffs and mountainsides; its call is a croak.

Redshank *Tringa totanus (Kokkinoskelis)*. Shy wader identifiable by its long red legs and bill; winter visitor to the lakes and Ropa valley marshes.

Robin *Erithacus rubecula (Kokkinolaimis)*. Needing no description, the robin sings throughout the year and feeds on insects, seeds and fruits.

Rock partridge *Alectoris graeca (Petroperdika)*. Slightly bigger than the common European partridge, this game-bird has a prominent black band at the base of its neck; rocky mountainsides.

Roller *Coracias garrulus (Chalkokourouna)*. Crow-like in size and call, this bird has dazzling blue and chestnut plumage; most often seen in northern Corfu, perched on telegraph wires.

Sand martin *Riparia riparia (Ochthochelidono)*. Brown and white bird with swallow-like wings; often seen in flocks while catching insects in flight; summer visitor.

Sardinian warbler *Sylvia melanocefala (Mavrotsirovakos)*. Darker than, but rather like the blackcap; its alarm note sounds like the winding of a clock.

Scops owl *Otus scops (Gionis)*. Very small (19 cm) owl with ear tufts; mainly active at night, repeatedly calling 'piu'. Widespread on Corfu, frequenting all habitats and preying on large insects.

Serin *Serinus serinus* (*Skarthaki*). Very small finch closely related to the canary; its jangling trill is heard in woodland areas.

Shag *Phalacrocorax aristotelis* (*Kormoranos*). Black sea bird with greenish sheen; flies only a metre above the sea and is often noticed when sitting on rocks, drying its outspread wings.

Shelduck *Tadorna tadorna* (*Varvara*). Large handsome duck with dark green head, white underparts and chestnut breastband. Winter visitor to salt water lagoons.

Skylark *Alauda arvensis* (*Korydadou*). Immediately recognisable by its airborne song and plummeting descent after sustained hovering.

Song thrush *Turdus philomelus* (*Kelaidotsichla*). Some are resident but their numbers are increased by migrants in winter; the song is tuneful but repetitive.

Squacco heron *Ardeola ralloides* (*Kryptotsiknias*). Small heron with light brown back, white wings and underside.

Stock dove *Columba oenas* (*Fassoperistero*). A native of northern Greece, resembling a small wood pigeon. Its call is a double 'coo' with the stress on the second 'syllable'.

Stonechat *Saxicola torquata* (*Mavrolaimis*). Black head, russet chest and white collar; haunts cliffs and open scrubland.

Swallow *Hirundo rustica* (*Stavrochelidono*). Spring migrant, many staying to nest. Blue-black on upper parts and pinkish beneath, its tail is conspicuously forked; catches insects in flight.

Swift *Apus apus* (*Mavrostachtara*). A summer visitor, this dark bird wheels and turns over towns and villages, squealing in flight. Best seen along the Mourayia (sea wall) in Corfu Town.

Teal *Anas crecca* (*Kirkiri*). This duck visits Corfu every winter and frequents the Andinioti lagoon; has a chestnut head with green 'eye-patch' outlined in white.

Water rail *Rallus aquaticus* (*Nerokotsela*). Nervous bird with brown back, grey face and barred flanks; lives in marshes and looks like a small moorhen.

White stork *Ciconia ciconia* (*Aspropelargos*). Enormous white bird with black-tipped wings; hunts frogs, lizards and small rodents over farmland and lakes. Summer visitor.

White wagtail *Motacilla alba alba* (*Lefkosousourada*). Small black and white bird with long wagging tail; closely resembles the British pied wag-tail and is similarly found near human settlement.

Wigeon *Anas penelope* (*Sfyrichtari*). The drake has a pink breast, buff crown and chestnut head; the rest of the plumage is grey. He whistles and the duck 'purrs'! Winter migrant.

Woodcock *Scolopax rusticola*. Striped brown bird with a long beak; in the mating season it performs a unique display flight known as 'roding'; hunted as game.

Wood pigeon *Columba palumbus* (*Fassa*). Endemic to Greece, this is the largest of the pigeons. Its call is very recognisable: 'coo-coo-coo-cooroo'.

Wren *Troglodytes troglodytes* (*Trochilos*). Minute brown bird with cocked tail; hunts insects and spiders in dry places.

Animals

Urban development, the construction of roads and hotel complexes and the replacement of natural vegetation by cultivated crops have driven many animals from their native habitats. Nevertheless, a considerable range of wildlife complements Corfu's rich flora: the island is, for example, one of the few places in Europe where the jackal (*Canis aureus*) is still found. It must be added that most people will not be lucky enough to see this animal as it is mainly nocturnal, very timid, and confines itself to the remoter mountain forests. Other wild mammals include hares, foxes, weasels, pine martens, hedgehogs – the eastern variety (*Erinaceus concolor*) – mice and bats. Dolphins, usually in smallish schools, may be spotted leaping from the waters of the Corfu channel or south towards Paxos. Seals are becoming rare but still colonise beneath the high Erimitis cliffs on Paxos.

Reptiles and Amphibians

In spring you are likely to see a wild tortoise (*Testudo hermanni*) emerging from the undergrowth or crawling across open ground; these are held in affection by the locals and are known as *cheloni*. Terrapins, toads and frogs proliferate in streams and pools and the green tree frogs croak loudly at night. The reddish-brown loggerhead turtle has become increasingly rare as touristic development of the beaches has progressed, but may still be seen swimming off the remoter shores.

Tortoise near Lake Korission

The island has an abundance of snakes and lizards: the great majority of the former are non-poisonous with the notable exception of the sand viper, Europe's most venomous snake (see p.39 for advice on snake bites). This creature (*Vipera ammodytes*) is mainly nocturnal, favours bare or rocky terrain, and can be recognised by a horn on the tip of its nose. Seek medical help if you fall foul of its bite. The Balkan whip snake (*Coluber gemonensis*) is light brown with darker speckles and a rather aggressive demeanour; it is common on Corfu and is not poisonous. Its relative, the large whip snake (*Coluber jugularis*), also harmless, is sandy brown with an orange underside. Often regarded as Europe's most beautiful snake, the leopard snake (*Elaphe situla*) is mottled in russet and silver. Equally identifiable is the 'four line' snake (*Elaphe quattuorlineata*) with four black lines running the whole length of its brown body. One of the larger snakes is the dice snake (*Natrix tessellata*) which is grey with darker markings and a yellow-orange stomach; it is generally common and lives in or near fresh water. Also preferring this habitat is the grass snake (*Natrix natrix*) which is greenish-grey with a bright yellow throat.

Despite the number of snakes occurring on Corfu, the walker is much more likely to encounter lizards. They bask on the steps of houses, on sunny rocks or on tree trunks, but often disappear once aware of an observer's proximity. Two of the larger species, the agama, resembling an iguana, and the luminiscent Balkan green lizard, tend to shy away from human habitation. The latter (*Lacertia trilineata*) is a most spectacular reptile, 30-40cm long and incredibly bright in colour. More common on the island is the Dalmatian algyroides (*Algyroides nigropunctatus*): the male has a distinctive blue throat and bright orange stomach. The Balkan glass lizard (*Ophisaurus adopus*) is large, thick and brown and often mistaken for a snake. The slow-worm (*Anguis fragilis*) is familiar throughout Europe and is long, thin and brown with tiny blue flecks. A nocturnal species, the Turkish gecko (*Hermidactylus turcicus*) is most likely to be spotted scaling the wall of a room and propelling itself across the ceiling with its adhesive fingers; it is light brown with dark speckles and is a useful fly catcher!

Insects

An island richly endowed with birds, plants and reptiles obviously supports abundant insect life. The more unusual butterflies include the Scarce Swallowtail (*Iphiclides podalirius*) which is paler than the Swallowtail and has longer 'tails' on the wings; the Cleopatra (*Gonepteryx cleopatra*) which resembles a Brimstone except that the male has a deep orange patch on the upper wings; and the Black-veined White (*Aporia crataegi*) whose name exactly describes its appearance.

From April until early June the nights are made magical by the sparking of fireflies: these are about a centimetre long and have flashing luminous tails in the mating season. Summer evenings are also alive with the chirping of crickets which sing in daylight too and resemble a long-legged beetle. In the olive groves the shriller song of the cicada is more likely to be heard: this large insect has huge transparent wings and clings to the trunks of trees. At ground level a large variety of beetles, ants and grasshoppers occur but they are usually unobtrusive. The most exotic of these must be the slender green praying mantis, one of Gerald Durrell's 'pets' in *My Family and Other Animals*. It may not be wise to investigate too thoroughly under stones in dry localities for this is the favoured habitat of the scorpion, a creative resembling a miniature lobster and carrying a painful sting in its upturned tail.

This is a rarely encountered 'nuisance'; the chief scourges to man are ants, horseflies, mosquitoes and wasps. Mosquitoes prevail at Andinioti lagoon, Lake Korission, Messongi beach, Agios Stefanos (N.E.), Agios Gordis beach and Alikes Potamou although they may be met elsewhere. A very effective mosquito killer, '*mikani gia ta kounoupia*', may be purchased in supermarkets and smaller shops all over the island. A plastic device, it is fed with pellets, then plugged into an electric socket: one pellet provides a night's protection. Similar appliances are on sale in the UK and USA. Wasps can be troublesome in the Barbati/Nissaki area but the rather alarmingly large, predominantly black Scoliid wasp is not in fact aggressive to humans. The also large, but much yellower, hornet has a sting which can be serious. The huge and rather fearsome-looking black bee with blue wings is not to be feared as it rarely stings: its presence in woods where it nests in dead branches gives it the name 'carpenter bee'.

HISTORY

To a considerable degree Corfu's turbulent history has been dictated by factors over which its inhabitants could have no control. Strategically sited at the entrance to the Adriatic, Corfu's distance from the Italian coast is only 74 km, and from the Albanian/Greek mainland a mere 2½ km.

From the beginning of its history, Kerkyra/Corfu has been a bridge and a bulwark (and sometimes a battleground) between East and West, the Roman world and the Greek, Christendom and Islam. Down the years, every emergent power in the Mediterranean, almost until our own century, has taken an acquisitive interest in the island. The result is a unique culture, perhaps as Italian as it is Greek, but displaying discernible legacies from many others of its successive occupants.

PREHISTORY AND MYTHOLOGY

Traces of human habitation on Corfu have been found (for example in cave dwellings at Gardiki, near Agios Mattheos in the south-west) that date back to the Paleolithic Age (70,000–40,000 years BC), a period at which it is thought the island may have been linked to Epirus on the Greek mainland, whence its first inhabitants would have come. In the fertile plain around Sidari fragments of tools and decorated Neolithic pottery (c. 6,000 BC) have been found, and at Afionas there have been Late Neolithic and early Bronze Age finds.

Of the tombs and other evidence of Mycenaean culture (17th–12th centuries BC) that are reasonably common on the more southerly Ionian islands, such as Zakynthos, Cefalonia and Levkas, Corfu shows no trace. The lack of such remains has led some historians to speculate that the island may have been in Phoenician hands during the Mycenaean period.

Whatever the facts about Corfu's prehistory, mythology has, since ancient times, firmly identified Corfu with Scherie, the 'land of shadowy mountains' 'far from the busy haunts of men' that was the home of the prosperous and civilized Phaeacians in Homer's *Odyssey*. Here Odysseus, *en route* from Calypso's isle Ogygia (probably Gozo off Malta), his ship destroyed by Poseidon's wrath and his comrades long since dispersed by the rigours of his ten-year voyage, was washed up naked and exhausted on a beach, to be found next day by Princess Nausicaa when she came with her handmaidens to do the palace washing at a nearby stream. After being fed, clothed and rested at the palace of Nausicaa's father, King Alcinous, Odysseus was taken in a Phaeacian galley and deposited still asleep on nearby Ithaca, his home island and the end of his epic journey. The city of the Phaeacians had 'an excellent harbour on each side' and was 'approached by a narrow causeway' – a description that fits three locations on Corfu: the Kanoni peninsula, Paleo-kastritsa and Afionas.

All these sites have had their adherents; all offer, moreover, a vaguely ship-shaped rock offshore (Pondiko-nissi or 'Mouse Island' off Kanoni, the rock of Kolovri off Paleokastritsa, and Gravia island – named from *karabia*, meaning 'ship' – north-west of Cape Arilla), which enthusi-asts have been able to link with the sequel to the story: that Poseidon, still incensed with Odysseus for the blinding of the Cyclops Polyphemus and resenting the Phaeacians' assistance to the hero, was permitted by Zeus to revenge himself by smiting their ship as it came within sight of home and turning it into a rock. As for the beach where Odysseus was washed up, Ermones, where a stream of sorts still flows into the back of the beach and which is more or less equidistant from Kanoni and Paleokastritsa, is usually favoured. Homer's Phaeacians and Scherie were doubtless intended to be magical and unreal, but the urge to identify places on Corfu with the *Odyssey* remains strong!

CORCYRA

Corfu's recorded history begins in 734 BC. In that year a party led by Chersicrates of Corinth founded a colony on the Kanoni peninsula. The new city, Corcyra (still preserved in the modern Greek name for Corfu, Kerkyra), arose on a site south of the modern town, in an area known to this day as Paleopolis ('Old City'). The acropolis was on the hill where today the village of Analipsis stands, behind city walls which linked Garitsa Bay with the Hyllaic harbour (today's Chalikiopoulos lagoon by the airport), which could be protected in times of danger by a chain stretching across its mouth to Perama. Much of the city probably lay in the grounds of what is now the villa of Mon Repos (see p.123).

From the outset the colony flourished. The Corfu channel offered the last refuge from westerly winds before ships embarked on the Adriatic crossing to southern Italy and Sicily, in both of which areas important Greek colonies were developing. Corcyra's position was therefore strategically invaluable. The city became rich; it maintained one of the most powerful navies in ancient Greece and from early in the sixth century BC minted its own coinage. In addition the island was fertile, Corcyraean wines in particular being famous throughout Greece. By 627 BC the colony had itself become a colonizing power, founding among other cities Epidamnus (modern Durres) in what is now Albania.

Corcyra's success soon brought it into conflict with its parent. As early as 664 BC the colony had defeated Corinth in the first recorded naval battle in history, and relations continued to be edgy until 435, when the cities found themselves supporting opposite sides in a civil conflict in Epidamnus. By now Corinth was a member of the Spartan alliance of Greek states and Corcyra felt compelled to ally itself with Athens against its mother city. It was this action of the Corcyreans which Thucydides saw as the prime cause of the ruinous Peloponnesian War, which was to last 27 years and is generally regarded as having brought the great era of classical Greece to an end.

Devastating for almost all the Greek city-states, the Peloponnesian War was a particular disaster for Corcyra, as Thucydides graphically describes. Before it, the island supported a vigorous colonial civilization with a population at its height of perhaps 100,000 (not unlike today). As a consequence of the war, a brutal civil conflict between democratic and oligarchical factions broke out; citizens were massacred and the state irrevocably weakened. In 338 BC Philip of Macedon finally defeated the Athenians and their allies at Chaeronea and from then on Corcyra, lacking allies, assumed a role that was to become familiar in the island's subsequent history – that of a strategic pawn fought over by powerful competing states from both east and west. A series of invasions followed, from Syracuse, Epirus, Illyria, and in 229 BC, the desperate islanders placed themselves under the protection of the new power in the Mediterranean, Rome.

Little remains of classical Corfu. The city on the Kanoni peninsula was extensively raided for its supplies of dressed stone when the medieval city was built on a site a little further north; later the Venetians (who are said to have removed some 20,000 stone blocks from Paleopolis) also found the area a convenient quarry when they were fortifying the city. Traces of temples have been found near the Kardaki spring and Mon Repos, elsewhere on the Kanoni peninsula and at Roda, and archaeological excavations may one day reveal more. The single most impressive classical artefact that survives is the Gorgon pediment from the sixth-century Temple of Artemis, now in the Archaeological Museum (see p.85).

Paleopolis church: a Corcyraean archbishop, Apollodorus, attended the Council of Nicaea in 325 – did he meet Spiridon of Cyprus there?

ROMAN CORFU (229 BC – 337 AD)

Corcyra was the first Greek city to come under Roman domination. The new colony once again thrived, becoming a major Roman naval base for their expansion into Macedonia and mainland Greece. Corcyra enjoyed over five centuries of relative tranquillity under the Romans, and was granted many privileges. The population increased and an impressive list of Roman notables visited the colony, which even then was a magnet for tourists: they included Cato, Cicero, Julius Caesar, Mark Antony and his enemy Octavius, and later the emperors Tiberius (who may have had a summer residence on the island), Nero (who performed at the temple of Jupiter Cassius at Kassiopi) and Titus.

Some time in the late first century SS Jason and Sosipater, disciples of St Paul, began the conversion of the island to Christianity. The oldest reminder of early Christianity on Corfu is the ruined sixth-century Paleopolis Church opposite the entrance to Mon Repos on the Kanoni peninsula. Remains of the Roman centuries, however, are few: apart from coins, the foundations of Roman buildings can be seen here and there (Moraitika, Kassiopi), and at Benitses and Paleopolis mosaics have survived, but otherwise there is little to show for five hundred years of, on the whole, benevolent rule.

BYZANTINE CORFU (337–1081 AD)

The emperor Diocletian's division of the Roman Empire

into western and eastern halves in 228 AD made it inevitable that, when in 337 AD the western half collapsed, Corfu should find itself part of the Byzantine empire, eventually forming a section of the *thema* of Cefalonia. Exposed and vulnerable at the western edge of Byzantium's domains, the island now resumed its historic role as strategic pawn. Piratical raids became the norm, and Corfu was devastated in turn by raiding Huns, Vandals, Ostrogoths (who completely destroyed the capital in 562) and Slavs. Most of the coastal settlements were abandoned, and the islanders took to living in the protectively huddled hill villages which are such a feature of the Corfiot countryside still. Following the Ostrogoth raid the capital was moved 2 km northwards, to the more defensible peaks on the promontory that is now the Old Fort.

NORMANS, SICILIANS AND ANGEVINS (1081–1386 AD)

Despite fairly constant strife, Byzantium managed to retain Corfu until 1081, when the island fell to an invasion by the Norman adventurer Robert Guiscard ('The Wizard'). He was subsequently ousted, as was a second Norman invasion in 1147 (this time the Byzantine forces were assisted by troops of a newly emergent power, Venice). Next the island was seized by Venice's arch rivals, the Genoese, under the freebooter Leone Vetrano.

In the opening years of the thirteenth century the infamous Fourth Crusade brought the shaky protection of Byzantium to an end. In 1203 a great fleet (its splendour is vividly described by the chronicler Villehardouin, who was present) assembled at Corfu and sailed, not as originally proposed to the Holy Land, but to Byzantium which was sacked and thoroughly looted. Thus the Empire was practically destroyed without a blow against the Infidel being struck. In the ensuing share-out the Venetians, due to the manipulative skills of the wily doge Dandolo, emerged with nominal control of crucial points along their trade routes to the Levant, including Crete, parts of the Peloponnese and the Ionian islands. In 1206 Corfu was finally wrested from Leone Vetrano and its government entrusted to a committee of Venetian nobles.

But Venice was unable to exert full control over all its new dominions immediately. The shock waves caused by the collapse of Byzantium took well over a century to settle, and during the next 150 years Corfu was passed from hand to hand. In 1214 Michael Angelos Comnenos, Despot of Epirus, an illegitimate member of the Byzantine imperial family who already controlled most of north-western Greece, seized the island from the Venetians; it was he who built the fortresses of Angelokastro and Gardiki on the west coast as a protection against Genoese pirates. In 1258 the island was once again taken, this time for King Manfred of Sicily. A brief return to Epirote control followed, then after his victory over the Sicilians at Benevento in 1266 Charles I of Anjou, King of Naples, became Corfu's overlord. This dynasty was to remain on Corfu for some 120 years. Although harsh, their rule brought a measure of stability and prosperity, but in the fourteenth century their power declined, and Corfu continued to be fought over, suffering constant incursions from Sicily, the Genoese and the Serbians. In 1386, in despair, a deputation of Corfiots (composed of two Greeks, two Italians and two Jews – an interesting reflection of the composition of the ruling classes at the time) formally appealed to the Doge of Venice for protection.

VENETIAN CORFU (1386-1797)

The Corfiot approach was warmly received, just as it had been by the Romans 1,600 years before. Venice fully appreciated the value of Corfu in securing her control of the Adriatic and in protecting her trading routes to the east. She bought the island from the Kingdom of Naples for 30,000 ducats, and in 1387 Corfu officially became part of the Venetian maritime empire, the *Stato da Mar*, of which it was to remain a part for 400 years.

Unlike previous occupants, the Venetians left their mark on the island; even today the Venetian legacy is responsible for many of its dominant characteristics. Corfu Town, in particular, with its tall buildings and narrow streets, its arcaded shops and palazzos, is typically Venetian: so is its relaxed way of life. In the countryside, too, there are gracious Venetian country houses, and the innumerable churches are almost all Italianate with separate belfries. But perhaps the greatest legacy of all are the olive trees which dominate the landscape (see p.77-8). The shift to olive production – previously Corfu's most celebrated product had been malmsey wine – permanently altered the island's economy.

As an important staging-post for east-west trade, Corfu prospered. No expense was spared in fortifying the island – in the sixteenth century it boasted 700 guns. The feudal system was maintained and the existing aristocracy reinforced – a Golden Book listing the nobility was begun in emulation of Venice's own *Libro d'Oro*, which by 1797, when Venice fell, contained 277 families (as late as 1925, when the last issue appeared, it still listed 24).

The peasantry fared less well. Heavily taxed and totally deprived of education, they were treated largely as serfs and chained to the soil by the demands of olive oil production (using technology that had not progressed since the Iron Age).

As part of the Venetian *Stato da Mar*, the main threat to Corfu came from the Turks, who had taken advantage of the vacuum created by the consequences of the Fourth Crusade to take Constantinople. In 1537 the notorious Barbary

Schulenberg's statue on the Esplanade: St Spiridon's annual procession on 11 August still pauses before it in grateful tribute

corsair Khair-el-Din (Barbarossa) attacked the island. He landed at Gouvia, razed Potamos and besieged Corfu Town. Under pressure from hunger and disease, the invaders retreated after two weeks, but not before 20,000 islanders had been killed or enslaved and the land ravaged. After this the canal was dug which separates the Old Fort from the town, and in 1570, just before Lepanto, work on the New Fort began, on the hill known as St Mark's.

The great naval victory at Lepanto in 1571, for which the international fleet assembled at Corfu and the island itself provided four ships and 1,500 men, crippled Ottoman maritime power. But Corfu remained vulnerable and in 1716 the Turks again invaded. By now Venice had lost Crete: therefore Corfu, 'the Gibraltar of Venice' in Jan Morris' phrase, had become its most important overseas possession. The island's defence was entrusted to the Saxon mercenary Count John Matthias von der Schulenberg. Despite landing 30,000 men (once again, mainly at Gouvia) the Turks were unable to take the city and after six weeks the coincidence of a daring sortie by Schulenberg's force (in which the townspeople and, tradition insists, St Spiridon himself joined in) and a violent freak thunderstorm so demoralised the invaders that they fled in disarray. Venice and the Corfiots were jubilant.

But, by the eighteenth century Venice, exhausted by the long struggle, was in decline. Indiscipline and corruption were rife, officials increasingly inept and self-indulgent. Corfu's wealth was systematically bled by its administrators (one *provveditore* even sold most of its military supplies to the Russians for his personal gain); the countryside had been ravaged by plague and after centuries of neglect was desperately impoverished and its people disaffected. By 1797, when Napoleon conquered Venice and Corfu became a French possession, even the famous fortifications had become dilapidated.

FRENCH AND RUSSIANS (1797–1814)

Corfu's new rulers saw the island as a priceless gain: Napoleon called it *'le clef d'Adriatique'* and pronounced its possession as 'of greater interest to us than all of Italy together'. Under the French the feudal system was abolished, educational facilities enhanced and the first printing press in Greece introduced. Corfu became a *département* of France with a seat in the Chamber of Deputies. But the Corfiots' initial enthusiasm for their new masters was short-lived. Taxes remained high, and the Orthodox Church was not respected; worse, the French garrison were poorly paid if at all and resorted to plunder. Thus, when a combined Russian-Turkish fleet ousted the French after a long siege in 1799, few tears were shed on the island. The following year the Ionian islands were officially constituted as the Heptanesian (or Septinsular) Republic, the first semi-independent Greek state since the fall of Constantinople in 1453. Nominally under the authority of the Turkish Sultan, the Republic was effectively a Russian protectorate. In 1807 the return of Napoleon and a *rapprochement* between France and Russia led to the Treaty of Tilsit, in which the Republic was dissolved and Corfu was once more ceded to France.

The second French period of occupation was also short, but considerably more benevolent. General François Donzelot, the French commandant, was a popular and capable governor. A large French garrison was based in Corfu and cultural and social life flourished. In 1808 an Ionian Academy was founded to foster science, the arts and crafts and commerce and the first School of Fine Arts opened a few years earlier. In Corfu Town the elegant arcades of the Liston were built along the Esplanade after the manner of the Rue de Rivoli in Paris, and in the countryside agricultural methods were improved.

Napoleon's abdication after Waterloo, however, led to the Congress of Vienna, at which a Russian proposal (instigated by Count John Kapodistrias, later to become modern Greece's first president, who attended as a Russian delegate) to grant independence to the Ionian islands was rejected by the other victorious powers. Finally, in the Treaty of Paris of 1815, it was resolved that the United States of the Ionian Islands should become a protectorate of the British, who had already been invited in by the southern islands and had taken Paxos the previous year.

THE BRITISH PROTECTORATE (1814–1864)

The First British Lord High Commissioner was Sir Thomas Maitland, known as 'King Tom'. Maitland was an unattractive character, shrewd and energetic, but uncouth, autocratic and often drunk. Since in his view the natives were unready for constitutional government he devised a new undemocratic constitution which left power firmly in his personal grip (and was roundly denounced for it by Kapodistrias). He also built the Palace of St Michael and St George, to function not only as his palace but also as the Senate House and as the headquarters of the new Order of the same name which he had founded to reward loyal Ionian islanders (and keep the nobility amenable).

The oldest official building in Greece, it was later to

become a palace for the Greek Royal Family. (Maitland was also governor of Malta, and used Maltese masons for the building work; a colony of Maltese was soon established on the island, which specialized in market gardening and of which remnants still survive.) 'King Tom' also commenced work on the construction of a road system all over the island – astonishingly, before the arrival of the British there seems to have been no wheeled traffic on the island at all. British soldiers were used for the work, and the occasional British milestone can still be seen beside some of the older roads which have not been widened since.

A vivid and often amusing account of life in British Corfu can be read in the letters of Private William Wheeler, of the 51st Battalion, Kings Own Yorkshire Light Infantry, who was stationed in the Ionians from 1823 to 1828. Certainly the culture and standards of Victorian Britain made a curious match with the elegant Mediterranean *dolce far niente* way of life on Corfu, and the comic potential of the situation was enhanced by a succession of colourful and eccentric Lord High Commissioners. But, in general, the representatives of the occupying power tended to live as a clique and mingle little with the natives – Edward Lear, for all his love of its natural beauty, found the island 'piggy-wiggy' and 'a very small, tittle-tattle kind of place'. One who enthusiastically took part in local life was the profoundly eccentric Lord Guilford, a fervent philhellene who was baptised into the Greek Orthodox faith and habitually wore classical Greek dress. He established the first university in Greece, the Ionian Academy, in 1824, bequeathing to it his own collection of some 25,000 books. His memory is still revered on the island, and he played an important part in making Corfu the chief literary and intellectual centre of Greece.

Nine Lord High Commissioners followed Maitland, who died (of apoplexy) in 1824. His successor, the cultivated Sir Frederick Adam, though vain and extravagant, was more popular with the Corfiots, one of whom became Lady Adam (despite having, as Wheeler tells us, 'a beard on her upper lip which would ornament a huzza'). As well as constructing the road to Paleokastritsa, a favourite spot of his (in order to justify the expense he first established a convalescent home for the military there), Adam also built the villa of Mon Repos; the house later became a royal residence, where Prince Philip, Duke of Edinburgh, was to be born. Most beneficially he arranged for the construction of an aqueduct from a spring above Benitses (where the waterworks can still be seen) which brought a permanent water supply to Corfu Town for the first time – before this

Sir Frederick Adam, rising appropriately from a pool of water, his most important gift to Corfu Town

water had come from the Potamos river on mule-back.

The islanders, however, increasingly chafed at their compulsory neutrality in the war of independence being waged by their brothers on the mainland against the Turks. After Greece became independent in 1827, pressure for *enosis* (unity) with the mainland increased, particularly after a later Commissioner, Sir Henry Ward, had put down an uprising in Cefalonia with great harshness in 1849. In 1858 William Gladstone undertook a special mission to the Ionian islands to investigate their disaffection and propose radical reforms in the constitution. Temporarily created Lord High Commissioner, he personally presented his proposals to the Legislative Assembly, but despite all his rhetoric the Ionians would accept nothing less than *enosis*, and on 16 February 1863 voted formally for secession from the protectorate and full union with Greece. After demolishing much of the old town's fortifications, the British withdrew 'with an air', *The Times* recorded, 'of generosity on one side and gratitude on the other seldom found in international transactions'.

The fifty years of the British protectorate brought the Ionian islands prosperity, not least by preserving them from the rigours of the war of independence being fought on the mainland. Besides the roads, waterworks and other useful legacies, the final abolition of the feudal system and (in 1852) the recognition of Greek as the official language, together with the intellectual and cultural advances encouraged by the foundation of the Academy, did much to equip the islands to play their full part in the new Greece. Other British legacies were more incongruous: they include the enduring popularity of cricket and Christmas pudding, and the availability on Corfu of *tsitsibira* (ginger beer)!

MODERN CORFU (1864 – THE PRESENT)

In October 1827 the battle of Navarino had brought mainland Greece independence from the Turks, and John Kapodistrias of Corfu was elected president. Many of his officials came from the Ionian islands, which now enjoyed a higher standard of living, education and political awareness than their mainland cousins. Kapodistrias was assassinated in 1831, however, and following a brief interregnum under Otho of Bavaria, the National Assembly in 1863 invited Prince William of Denmark to become King George I of the Hellenes. For Britain this was an acceptable choice, permitting the surrender of its Ionian protectorate as a gesture of goodwill to the new king, and the treaty of 29 March 1864 formalized the cession.

For Greece the acquisition of the Ionian islands, while enthusiastically welcomed, posed economic problems: Britain's insistence on their remaining neutral prevented Greece from using them as naval bases, and the costs of administering the islands often outweighed the revenues they provided. Corfu continued to prosper for a while, but, faced for the first time with earning its own living in the world without the support of a wealthy foreign power, the island fell into decay. A glimpse of the future, however, was provided by the increasing number of leisured and wealthy visitors from other parts of Europe who began to visit the island, attracted by its climate and natural beauty. As early as the 1850s, the British had been coming, and in the years before World War I many of the larger country houses were occupied by 'tourists'. Mon Repos became a summer residence for the Greek royal family, and in the 1890s the Achilleion was built for Elizabeth of Austria, the beautiful and tragic wife of Franz Josef. After Elizabeth's assassination in 1898 the palace was eventually purchased by Kaiser Wilhelm II of Germany.

Officially neutral in the First World War, Corfu was nevertheless used as a naval base by the British, French and Italian allies. In 1916 the island was host to the exiled government of Serbia and some 150,000 troops after the Austrians had driven them from the mainland – the parliament met in the town theatre. Unfortunately a large number (perhaps as many as 50,000) of the Serbian troops died from disease, overcrowding and the rigours of the retreat: many are buried in the Serbian cemetery on Vidos island. Before their departure the Serbs signed the Declaration of Corfu (1917), which laid the foundations of modern Yugoslavia.

After the war, disputes over the Greek-Albanian frontier, always a contentious issue, precipitated the 'Corfu Incident' of 1923, when the Italian delegate to the commission held to discuss the matter was assassinated by an unknown hand on Greek soil. The Italians under Mussolini retaliated by bombarding Corfu and occupying the island, provoking the first international crisis to confront the fledgeling League of Nations. In due course the Italians were persuaded to hand back the island, but not before Greece had paid a large indemnity.

In 1941-3 the Italians were back on Corfu, having invaded Greece from Albania. An Italian governor was appointed, and in one respect the occupation benefited the island: the plain of the Ropa river was drained and properly irrigated to become one of Corfu's most important agricultural areas. Following the Anglo-Italian armistice in 1943, however, the island was unable to repel a landing by the Germans and after ten days of damaging bombardment the Nazis took Corfu, exacting cruel reprisals on the captured Italians (some 5,000 of whom may have been murdered). In 1944 Corfu was liberated by the Allies; but only a few months before the German evacuation the Jewish population of some 4,000 had been herded into the Old Fort before being shipped off to an unknown destination – only 80 returned after the war. The bombardments of the Second War did terrible damage to Corfu Town, over a quarter (perhaps 500 buildings) of which was destroyed, including the Ionian Parliament, the theatre, Lord Guilford's library and many churches.

Corfu was not greatly affected by the Greek civil war which followed, but since the war the island's fortunes have been those of modern Greece. The only invaders have been tourists, who have brought change but also prosperity, so that today Corfu is one of the wealthiest and fastest-developing areas of Greece.

Economy and industry

AGRICULTURE AND FISHING

Despite the importance of tourism, agriculture remains the paramount industry on Corfu, employing over 60 per cent of the population. At about 120 people per sq. km (almost twice the national average) the island's rural population density is the highest in Greece, and the land is more fertile than most areas of the country. Nevertheless the rural population has been shrinking steadily for some years, as people turn from the land to become shop-keepers, waiters or construction workers.

Altogether about 59 per cent of the island's area is cultivated, over half of it with **olive** trees, which are mentioned on Corfu by Homer but have probably been grown on the island for five thousand years. Their numbers grew dramatically under the Venetians, who bribed the peasantry to plant as many olive trees as their land could bear. By the end of the seventeenth century there were two million on Corfu and a family's wealth was estimated by the number of trees it owned: today there are an estimated 3,500,000.

The Corfiot tradition is neither to prune the branches of the olive nor to pick the fruit; consequently the trees grow to gigantic proportions and the ripe olives are allowed to fall to the ground. Legend has it that St Spiridon, appearing in an olive grove, advised the landowner that cutting or beating the trees was cruel, and a saying has grown out of this myth that Corfiot men 'beat neither their olive trees nor their women'. The religious connection continues, with some families choosing to bequeath single olive trees to the Church: the fruits from these are never gathered but lie rotting on the ground, belonging only to God. A benediction is still sought from the local priest before the oil-

Plastic netting spread semi-permanently under the olive trees has made the lot of the peasant farmer somewhat easier

pressing begins, and the little lights in the wayside shrines are fuelled with olive oil.

Elsewhere in Greece the olives are picked or the trees beaten so that the fruit falls into plastic nets spread out beneath the trees. Nets are also arranged under the trees in Corfu, but only to catch the naturally falling olives: these ripen in winter, and the netting remains in place from November to June, to cover the entire ripening period. The older women usually gather the fruits, and they may sometimes be heard singing traditional songs as they work; by ancient custom they are often allowed by the owners to bring their animals with them to browse under the trees.

Olives are 'for the peasant a good servant and a hard master', as Lawrence Durrell put it. The trees take seven to twelve years to bear their first crop and thereafter produce a full crop only in alternate years. There are olive groves on all but the steepest slopes in Corfu and almost everybody owns at least a few trees (which can, in fact, be owned independently of the land on which they grow, a complication which has caused problems for property developers from time to time!)

Olives destined for oil-making are put into barrels which are positioned by the roadside and collected at intervals to be taken to the presses. Nowadays these are electric, but only thirty years ago the ancient method of crushing the fruit between circular stones was still practised in the villages. The stones, a perpendicular revolving on a horizontal, were turned by horses walking round and round for hours on end. Abandoned presses (*litrouvia*) may still be seen lying around in farmyards and derelict buildings.

Though olive oil was almost the sole agricultural product of the island until the Second World War, a wide variety of other crops are now grown. Only a small proportion of the land is irrigated, most of it in the Ropa Plain (a great marsh until the Italians drained it during the Second War), in the valley of the Messonghi river and around the Chalikiopoulos lagoon.

After olives, the main crops are **vines** and **cereals**, of both of which the Ropa Plain is an important producer. Citrus fruit (including *koumkouats* for making the popular local liqueur) are grown in sheltered areas around Benitses, Potamos and Lefkimmi, and peaches, apricots, apples, pears, cherries, figs and melons are also produced, as are nuts, including almonds, walnuts and carob. Among vegetables, onions, tomatoes, green beans, cucumbers and artichokes all have their place in the farmer's repertoire, and there are small crops of tobacco, sugar beet, peanuts and sunflower seeds.

Not much of the land offers good pasture for livestock; nevertheless there are plenty of flocks of sheep and goats on the island. **Fishing**, although no longer an important industry, is still practised in the traditional way. Fishermen mostly work at night, using acetylene lamps, and often a single large net which is cooperatively owned.

INDUSTRY

About a third of Corfu's population is employed in industry or services. The once important **salt** industry is now confined to the salt flats on Cape Lefkimmi in the extreme south. Other industries include food and drink processing, and there are small concerns making footwear, textiles and leather goods. **Construction**, riding on the back of tourism, is the source of a great deal of employment.

Tourism and its associated services have since the 1950s become ever more important on Corfu; successive Greek governments have made loans to encourage investment in the industry and the island is now one of the most popular resorts in Greece, particularly with the British.

The intensively farmed Ropa Plain: hedges and walls are rare in Corfu

CULTURE AND FOLKLORE

Architecture

The churches of Corfu, of which there are said to be about 800, are almost all Italianate in design.

Easily their most distinctive feature is the separate bell tower: this is either a campanile, topped by a dome or pyramid over a balcony (St Spiridon's and the churches at Potamos and Argirades have fine examples), or a much simpler affair: a thick whitewashed free-standing wall which tapers to a point over a space in which one or two bells hang. These charming structures can be seen everywhere: often they are decorated with coloured lights or tiers of potted plants.

In the countryside the Italian influence is also displayed in the stuccoed mansions of the wealthy which although often crumbling nowadays still retain a faded elegance. A visit to Old Perithia (see p.135-6) offers a good opportunity to examine the distinctive Corfiot/Venetian style of domestic architecture, preserved from the late eighteenth century.

Among secular buildings, the most dramatic in Corfu are the work of military architects: the massive hulks of the two fortresses in the town and the citadels of Angelokastro, Kassiopi and Gardiki. Notable among post-Venetian contributions to the townscape are the Liston (built by the French) and the British-built neoclassical Palace of St Michael and St George, regarded by the diplomat and diarist Harold Nicolson as the finest example of the Regency style outside Britain.

Art

Corfiot art, like its architecture, has been influenced by both east and west. The fall of Constantinople dispersed that city's artistic community, many of them to Crete, where a less strict style of painting developed under the influence of Renaissance ideas from western Europe. As the chief link between Crete and Venice, Corfu was soon to see the development of a similar movement away from mannered Byzantine formality; moreover, following the loss of Crete to the Turks in the seventeenth century, many members of the Cretan School settled in the Ionians, bringing their more realistic techniques with them and producing icons and wall-paintings with a greater understanding of composition and perspective than the tradition had previously allowed.

Important Cretan painters who worked on Corfu include **Michael Damaskinos** (who had taught El Greco), and later **Theodoros Poulakis** and **Emmanuel Tzanes**. **Panagiotis Doxaras** (1662–1729) may be regarded as the

Corfu belfry: centuries of rule by Roman Catholics caused a withering of the Greek tradition in the Ionians and the emergence of a distinctive local style

founder of an Ionian School of painting: the ceiling panels in St Spiridon's church, now largely painted over, were his work. His son Nicholas maintained a tradition which was carried on by two priests from Zakynthos, **Nicholas Koutouzis** (1741-1813) and **Nicholas Kandounis** (1767-1834), who studied in Venice and adopted western techniques wholeheartedly.

Most of the frescoes and painted ceilings from this period have not survived, but there are fine icons in many churches, both in Corfu Town and around the island; there is also a representative collection in the Byzantine Museum (see p.85). Later Corfu produced the sculptor **Pavlos Prosalendis**, who was a pupil of Canova and established the island's first School of Fine Arts in 1805. The statues of Kapodistrias, Sir Frederick Adam and Lord Guilford around the Esplanade are all his work.

Literature

Under the Venetians Corfu's first literary society, the *Accademia degli Assicurati*, was founded in 1656; among its members was an early historian of Corfu, **Andreas Marmoras**. In the following century the island produced two priests, **Evgenios Voulgaris** and **Nikiforos Theotokis**, who were influential men of letters, writing in Greek at a time when the educated classes customarily wrote and read Italian. The arrival of the first printing press under the French produced a surge of literary endeavour: new literary and educational societies sprang up and newspapers and pamphlets were published on the island. Lord Guilford's foundation of the Ionian Academy in 1824, and his provision of a library, gave another boost to intellectual life, one which was to benefit Greece generally.

But it was the presence on Corfu of the poet **Dionysios Solomos** (1798-1857) from 1828 until his death that most stimulated cultural life on the island, to the extent that Corfu became the intellectual centre of Greece. Born in Zakynthos, Solomos was the first Greek writer to write in the everyday 'demotic' language of the people, elevating it to a genuinely poetic medium. This was a revolutionary step, which was to lead to the formation of a literary movement, the Corfu Literary School, which insisted on the need for literature to be written in a language that ordinary people could read. Solomos wrote many celebrated poems: the best-known is his patriotic *Hymn to Freedom* (1823), part of which was adopted to form the Greek national anthem. Several of Solomos' disciples became well known, among them the critic and translator **Iakovas Popylas**, the poet

The eccentric Earl of Guilford: dissuaded from founding his Ionian Academy in Ithaca, he won the undying affection of the Corfiots

Gerasimos Markoras and the Ithacan patriotic poet, **Lorenzos Mavilis**.

Ironically, the flowering of literature in the early nineteenth century, which the British encouraged, had the effect of focusing Greek patriotism and encouraging the growth of an intelligentsia, both of which played a part in helping to undermine the British protectorate.

Music and Dance

Corfu is renowned for its town bands, with their colourful uniforms and plumed helmets; several country villages maintain one, and there are at least three in Corfu Town. It has been estimated that as many as 10,000 islanders play an instrument, and from 21 May onwards there are regular concerts on the bandstand on the Esplanade (enquire at the Tourist Office for details). Corfu also has a Philharmonic Orchestra and Choir.

In 1840 the island's first music school, the Philharmonic Society, was founded by the Corfiot composer **Nikolaos Mantzaros** (1795-1874) – later to be chosen to arrange Solomos' words to music for the Greek national anthem. Honorary members of the Society have included Gounod and Rossini.

Otherwise popular music on Corfu today follows the rest of Greece. Visitors may well hear the famous *bouzouki* in some of the tavernas on the island – in fact this 'typically Greek' mandolin-type instrument originates in Asia Minor and only arrived in Greece in the 1920s. They are also extremely likely to see (and be invited to join in) the *syrtaki*, the slow but accelerating dance traditionally performed by two to twenty men standing side by side with their arms over each other's shoulders.

An important event in the cultural year is the Corfu International Festival (Aug–Oct) of concerts, opera and ballet held in the Theatre and the Old Fortress (information and programmes from posters in the town, the Tourist Office or phone 39528).

Museums

Museum of Asiatic Art, Palace of St Michael and St George
Open daily 8.30–15.00, closed Mondays: 400 dr. (tel: 23124)

This unusual museum is based on a collection of 10,000 Oriental artefacts left to the state by the diplomat Grigorios Manos; subsequent donations have been added to form one of the most comprehensive collections of Asian art in the world. It comprises ceramics, silks, netsuke, armour, screens and objects made of ivory, bronze, stone, lacquer and clay; countries represented include China, Korea, Japan, Nepal, India, Thailand and Tibet. In the same wing of the Palace is a collection of Christian art, including mosaic fragments from Paleopolis, scraps of fresco and a selection of icons from the sixteenth to eighteenth centuries, including examples by Damaskinos, Poulakis and Tzenos.

The terrifying Gorgon flanked by 'leopanthers'; 17 m long and originally brightly coloured, the pediment is an important example of the stylized sculpture of archaic Greece

The staterooms of the Palace itself are worth seeing in their own right; as well as containing displays of Oriental artefacts they offer painted ceilings, portraits, some magnificent marble fireplaces and good sea views.

Archaeological Museum 5 Vraila St. Open daily 08.30–15.00, closed Mondays: 200 dr. (tel: 30680)

Housed in a well-lit modern building, the museum is not well signposted: it is reached either by taking Mantzarou St from near San Rocco Square and making for the waterfront; or by following the coast southwards from the Esplanade past the Corfou Palace Hotel then turning inland at the next block. Its outstanding attraction is the celebrated 'Gorgon Pediment', a sensitively restored archaic work of *c.* 580 BC from the temple of Artemis in Paleopolis which is the oldest surviving monumental sculpture in Greece. The figure of a recumbent lion displayed next door was found near the Tomb of Menecrates; made by an unknown Corinthian sculptor, this is artistically one of the finest pieces in the museum.

Other exhibits include funerary monuments from the ancient cemetery at Garitsa, early Neolithic artefacts from Sidari, pieces from the temple near Roda, and fragments (heads of lions and women) from the temple of Hera, ancient Corcyra's major centre of worship. Photography is allowed in the museum on payment of an extra charge.

The *Byzantine Museum* is housed in the sixteenth-century church of Antivouniotissa at the top of a flight of steps leading from Arseniou St on the sea wall. It contains icons and other paintings from the sixteenth, seventeenth and eighteenth centuries. Open 08.45–15.00 Tues to Sun, 400 dr., but closed for restoration at the time of writing.

Other museums include the *Solomos Museum* (memorabilia associated with the poet) in Arseniou St (Mon–Fri 18.00–21.00, no charge) and the *Paper Money Museum* housed upstairs in the Ionian Bank off N. Theotoki St in 'Ioniki Square'. (09.00–13.00 Mon to Sat, 10.00–12.00 Sun, no charge.)

Danilia Village (see p.98) has a folk museum with a collection of old household effects and agricultural implements.

In connection with museums it should be noted that antiquities may not be exported without a licence from the Greek Archaeological Service. If you buy anything ancient it is essential to obtain an export permit from the dealer; and should you find any antiquity (anywhere, including in the sea), do not attempt to take it home without informing the authorities as the penalties for smuggling such items are severe.

Festivals

Almost every town and village on Corfu has at least one *panagiros*, a festival in celebration of the saint's day of the local church. After a special service, an icon or other religious totem will be paraded around the streets in a colourful procession, after which there will be eating, drinking and dancing out of doors, in all of which strangers are welcome to join. The best known *panagiros* is that of the Pantokrator, held from 3–6 August at the monastery on top of the mountain: hundreds of islanders used to flock to this festival from all over Corfu and spend at least one night there in cells around the church.

St Spiridon

In Corfu Town festive occasions frequently revolve around the island's much-loved patron saint, St Spiridon, in whose honour no less than four processions are held annually. Spiridon was a Cypriot shepherd (from Trimithion, near Nicosia) who rose to become bishop of a minor country diocese and in 325 attended the Council of Nicaea, which promulgated the Nicene Creed and the doctrine of the Holy Trinity. (On the way he performed a famous miracle after his mules had been beheaded one night by a party of rival delegates: in the dark he ordered his attendants to replace the mules' heads on their bodies, whereupon they came alive again – only in daylight was it found that a white mule had been given a brown head and vice versa!) Numerous other miracles were attributed to him and after his death a sweet odour arose from his grave: when exhumed, his body was found to be perfectly preserved. Venerated as a saint, Spiridon's mummy stayed at Trimithion until removed to Constantinople to protect it from Saracen raids.

Just before the Turks captured Constantinople in 1453 a wealthy priest named Kalocheiritis acquired Spiridon's remains and those of St Theodora Augusta and conveyed them through Epirus to Corfu slung in sacks on either side of a mule. Here St Theodora was in due course donated to the community – she now rests in Corfu cathedral. St Spiridon's relics, however, proved a lucrative asset for the Kalocheiritis family and were handed down by inheritance until they passed to the Voulgaris family as part of the dowry of a female descendant. In 1598 the saint was placed in his own church, where he remains to this day: a shrivelled form reposing in a glass-fronted casket from which his tiny feet, encased in embroidered slippers, protrude at the bottom to be kissed by the faithful.

Among a host of minor cures and miracles, St Spiridon is believed to have rescued the population from disaster on at least four occasions: in 1629 and 1673 he dispersed plagues that were ravaging the island, in 1553 he averted famine and, most momentously, in 1716 he appeared during a dramatic thunderstorm and helped to put the besieging Turkish armies to flight. These are the occasions which his four annual processions (on Palm Sunday, Easter Saturday, 11 August and the first Sunday in November) commemorate. On each of them, the gilt casket containing his mummified remains is carried on silver poles by priests and paraded around the streets and the Esplanade, accompanied by the Metropolitan of Corfu and a procession of civic dignitaries, soldiers and school children, to the accompaniment of solemn music from one of the town bands. His own name day is 12 December, when his casket is stood upright in the church so that the faithful may kiss his slippers.

In Lawrence Durrell's words, 'The island is really the Saint and the Saint is the island'. As recently as 1944 St Spiridon saw to it that his church and all those who took refuge in it survived the devastating German bombardment. The saint's influence remains powerful in the life of the island he protects: people swear by him and well over half the male children on Corfu are named Spiro after him!

Easter on Corfu
Easter (*Pascha*, but on Corfu often called '*Lambri*' – literally 'brilliance') is the biggest event in the island's calendar, and visitors from many other parts of Greece come to attend the spectacular celebrations. These begin on Good Friday,

when every church mounts a procession through the flag-hung streets, accompanied by a contingent from one of Corfu's town bands playing solemn music. The day's climax is reached after dark, when, bearing crosses of flowers, the main procession sets off from the cathedral, led by the Metropolitan and accompanied by subdued music from the bands.

Holy Saturday brings the most splendid procession of all, that of Saint Spiridon. The saint's remains are paraded from his church to the Esplanade and back, accompanied by the Metropolitan in splendid blue and gold vestments, local dignitaries, school children and the band of the St Spiridon Philharmonic Society. Then, at 11.00 a.m., the streets are cleared for the celebrated 'breaking of the pots', and suddenly a shower of unwanted crockery, plates, flower-pots, vases – anything that can be noisily smashed – is hurled into the streets from the upper windows of the houses. The origin of this ancient and peculiar custom is unknown: quite possibly it descends from a medieval custom reflecting the treatment meted out to any Jews who rashly ventured out of the ghetto during Holy Week. The pot-smashing lasts only a few minutes, after which people pour out into streets now ankle-deep in pottery fragments; for obvious reasons, partially arcaded streets such as N. Theotoki and Evg. Voulgareos are popular spots for watching the ritual!

The climactic moment of the festivities comes on the stroke of midnight on the Esplanade, when the Metropolitan pronounces '*Christos anesti*' ('Christ is risen!') from the bandstand. Immediately, the bands strike up, church bells ring, ships hoot from the harbour and fireworks soar from the Old Fort; meanwhile each of the many thousands of onlookers lights a candle before going home to break his or her fast with special crimson-dyed Easter eggs and feasting.

Other Festivals

1 January *Protochronia* or St Basil's Day: public holiday; children (and the traffic police!) receive presents; a sprig of basil may be offered to strangers.

6 January Epiphany (*ton Theofanion*): public holiday; the Metropolitan blesses the sea, throwing a cross into the waters of the harbour, whence it is retrieved by the nimblest of a crowd of small boys.

25 March Greek Independence Day: public holiday and processions in the town.

Clean Monday *Kathari Deftera* (Shrove Monday), the first day of Lent for the Orthodox church; families fly kites, picnic in the country and only seafood, greens, olives and special flat bread is eaten – also *chalva*, a honeyed sweet.

1 May Labour Day: wreaths of flowers are displayed on front doors and everyone makes for the countryside.

21 May Ionian Union Day (*Enosis ton Heptanisson*) marks the anniversary of the Ionian Islands' joining the Kingdom of Greece in 1864: wreath-laying, a fly-past, cannons booming, bands and parades.

12 December *Agiou Spiridonos* St Spiridon's Day: all the Spiros on Corfu receive gifts and the body of the saint is displayed upright in his church.

There are also the four days when St Spiridon is celebrated with processions through Corfu Town (see p.86–7).

Sun-drenched corner, Vatos

SPORTS AND ACTIVITIES

Sports

CANOEING

Canoes may be hired from the Top Sail Club, Glifada Beach (tel. 94201/2), at Benitses, Perama, Sidari, Paleokastritsa or from the Nautical Club of Corfu near the Corfou Palace Hotel in Garitsa Bay. This club also offers rowing, water polo and underwater fishing.

CRICKET

Cricket was brought to Corfu in the nineteenth century by the British and has been played in the capital ever since. The game itself was known on the island as *play*: runs are still called *ronia* and *owdat* (a corruption of 'how's that?') means 'out'. Nowadays the game's popularity is in decline and the majority of regular spectators on Wednesdays, Saturdays and Sundays are middle-aged or elderly. The pitch is on the Esplanade opposite the Liston (see town map) and matches usually start at 14.45. Throughout September a cricket festival is held, featuring visiting teams which include sides from Britain and Malta who pit their skills against the two Corfiot clubs, Byron and Gymnastikos. Holidaymakers wishing to participate should ask their hotel receptionist or the tourist office to make arrangements or telephone the clubs (Byron: tel: 39504; Gymnastikos: tel: 38726).

Cricket in the shadow of the Old Fort: the quaint cricketing terms used locally include the Italian-influenced *balloni* (balls), *tapetto* (wicket) and *fermadoros* (wicket-keeper)

DIVING

The deep water off the west coast of Corfu is remarkably clear and affords excellent visibility for divers. Limestone caves penetrate the cliffs of the Paleokastritsa area and harbour an interesting variety of Mediterranean fish.

The diving school at Paleokastritsa (Barracuda Club) is more than 25 years old and has professional instructors. Experienced divers may also use their boats. There are smaller schools at Ermones Beach and Agios Gordis: on the east coast there is the Waterhoppers Scuba Diving Centre at Ipsos (tel: 93532 after 18.00). All these clubs welcome beginners.

Before enrolling at a diving centre, you will require a certificate of health which is obtainable from doctors on Corfu. *N.B It is dangerous to fly less than 48 hours after diving.*

FISHING

There are no restrictions on where to fish around Corfu's coasts. Fish are so abundant that the amateur usually feels well rewarded at the end of a session. Local boatmen are often willing to take small groups out and such trips should be negotiated privately at the quayside. Underwater fishing expeditions can be arranged with the Nautical Club of Corfu in Garitsa Bay.

GOLF

Corfu's golf club is situated in the Ropa Valley, 15km west of Corfu town and 1.5km from Ermones Beach: the 6800 yard course has 18 holes, 3 sets of tees and a par of 72. It is said to be among the finest in the Mediterranean and has the added facilities of a practice ground and putting green. A complex watering system keeps the whole course efficiently irrigated throughout the summer but golfers may sometimes regret this facility: a capriciously winding stream is an obstacle on all but two of the holes!

The modern clubhouse, attractively built of local stone, has a luxurious bar and restaurant. Lessons may be booked with qualified professionals.

Green fees in 1990 were around 4000 dr. per day or 20,000 dr. per week. For more up-to-date information, write to Corfu Golf and Country Club, PO Box 17, Corfu or telephone them on 94220/1.

Some of the island's more exclusive hotels offer a courtesy coach service to the club.

HUNTING

Many Corfiots are keen hunters and shoot small birds 'for the pot' as well as water fowl and hares. A favourite target is the woodcock which is stewed in wine to make a traditional dish known as *bikatsis krassatas*. Recently more birds have become protected by the Greek government in response to pressure from conservation groups.

Before contemplating hiring a gun or shooting, remember that a licence is necessary. This can be obtained from the Greek Federation of Hunting Societies, Korai St 2, Athens (tel: 3231271); alternatively a permit for two weeks only can be issued by the Forestry Department through the Tourist Police in Plateia Eleftherias, Corfu Town (tel: 30265).

PARASAILING

This sport has become exceedingly popular on Corfu and is offered at the following beaches: Kontokali, Gouvia, Dasia (Spiro's Ski Club – tel: 33871), Pyrgi (Dino's Ski Club – tel: 93325), Liapades, Glifada (Top Sail Club – tel: 94201), ·Agios Gordis, Kavos and Messongi.

RIDING

A maze of bridleways makes riding very enjoyable on Corfu. Treks and instruction for beginners may be booked at any of these equestrian establishments: Kerkyra Golf Hotel (adjacent stables and paddock), Alikes Potamou (tel: 31785/7); Grecotel Corcyra Beach, Gouvia (tel: 30770/1/2); Barrique Riding Stables, Afra (tel: 52143). This last riding school is in the centre of the island, north of the main road from Corfu Town to Pelekas.

Riding is also possible at Kassiopi: enquire locally. All these stables are open from April to October, usually during the early mornings and early evenings to avoid the heat.

SAILING

Endowed with 217 km of coastline, Corfu is a favourite among yachtsmen. Besides the natural attractions of rugged inlets, glorious beaches and enticing harbours, the island is well equipped with berthing facilities.

Before setting sail for Corfu, it is wise to obtain Rod Heikell's *The Greek Waters Pilot* (published by Imray, Laurie, Norie and Wilson, London); also the relevant British Admiralty charts. On arrival, the official ports of

Small sailing craft at anchor, Paleokastritsa

entry are Corfu Port, Dasia and Gouvia. The Port Authority
will require the ship's log for inspection and a customs
officer will issue a 'transit log' to be retained while the boat
is in Greek waters. This is valid for six months, then
renewable annually thereafter. A courtesy Greek flag
should be flown. The 'transit log' authorises the crew and
passengers to go ashore during the day but they must spend
each night aboard the vessel unless their passports have
been endorsed by the immigration authorities.

From April to October the weather is mainly dry with
reliable light breezes blowing from the south-east in April,
May, September and October, from the west in June and
veering to north-west in July and August. The *maestro* or
summer north-westerly tends to be an afternoon wind,
dying at sunset: it can be gusty. The passage through the
narrow channel between NE Corfu and Albania can be
difficult and is probably best negotiated with a following
wind.

Greek radio and television issue frequent weather fore-
casts including special bulletins for shipping. From Monday to Friday these are broadcast in English at 06.30 local
time on 729 kHz(AM) from Athens but are more easily
picked up on Corfu's radio station on 1008 kHz(AM); this
also has a daily forecast in English at 07.30 GMT. Special
gale warnings to yachts are broadcast on VHF Channel 16
at 07.03, 09.03, 11.33, 17.03 and 23.03 local time. A shipping
forecast may be obtained by telephone at any time from the
Hellenic National Meteorological Service on Athens
8940616.

Corfu's major yacht marina is at Gouvia, with 350 berths

(PO Box 29, 49100 Corfu or tel: 0661-91475/91376). It is 8km by road (bus service) to the port in Corfu Town where there are more berths, repair facilities, ship's chandlers and all other conveniences. Garitsa Bay, south of the Old Fort, has plentiful moorings. On the west coast, fuel and shelter are obtainable at Paleokastritsa.

Yacht chartering has become very popular in the Greek islands. Sailing and motor yachts vary from the fairly basic to the large and luxurious. They can be hired with or without crew but, in the latter case, the charterer must hold a proficiency certificate from a recognised yacht club. A list of charter yachts may be obtained from the Association of Boat and Yacht Rental Agents, PO Box 341, Piraeus.

Flotilla cruising is also big business: two companies operating in the Ionian Sea are Leisure Villas (071-540-5720) and Flotilla Sailing Holidays (081-969-5423 or, on Corfu, 0661-22018). Also on the island is Salvanos Travel (tel: 34050).

Several harbours offer sailing dinghies for hire by the week: expect to pay around £150 per week for a Laser and substantially less for a Hobby 12. A limited number of Sailord 300s are available for children and teenagers. All these, by law, carry life-jackets and flares, but should *never* be taken out by the uninitiated.

The Greek National Tourist Office publishes a useful booklet, *Sailing the Greek Seas*, which is obtainable from their offices in Corfu Town, in the UK and in the USA (see p.35).

In August, the Nautical Association (NAOK) holds a regatta and boat race on the sea front below the Kapodistrias statue with traditional music and singing by moonlight.

SWIMMING

All types of swimming may be enjoyed on Corfu. From a boat, the small caves and offshore rocks of the west coast are exciting to explore if you have snorkelling equipment. This can easily be purchased on the island. Equally rewarding for this sport are the weedy shallows of the east where the water is much warmer and the eel grass conceals an amazing variety of small fish.

The sea is cleanest on the west coast but the water temperature is appreciably cooler. The best sandy beaches are also on this side, with the exception of the long strand at Kavos in the far south-east. There are few currents to make swimming hazardous but it should be noted that lifeguards are a rarity. A warning flag may be red or black – observe either! The shallows of Gouvia, Sidari, Roda and Kavos are

Pedaloes at Dasia

particularly safe for children but less suitable for serious swimmers. Bathing in the vicinity of Corfu Town, notably in the port area and at Garitsa Bay, should be avoided because of pollution.

As it is technically illegal in Corfu to have a private beach, swimming is permissible from any point along the coastline. Access to a beach, however, may well be through private land, thereby making it impossible to reach except from the sea.

TENNIS

The 95-year-old Corfu Tennis Club, the oldest in Greece, is at 4 Romanou St, not far from the Archaeological Museum. It has four asphalt courts which are only hired out to the public between 08.00 and 12.00 but lessons are available as are racquet hire and changing room facilities (tel: 37021). A newer club at Kefalamandouko on the road above the New Port also offers coaching.

Many hotels have their own tennis courts with equipment for hire.

WALKING

A vast network of mule tracks and footpaths crisscrosses Corfu; the walker is thus able to get much more of an idea of Corfiot life than is possible from a car. Obviously these paths cross private land and are not necessarily 'rights of way' although prohibitive signs are rare. It is of course courteous to keep strictly to the tracks and not to risk damaging any olive nets by walking over them. If the landowner or his workers are around, you will usually get a friendly welcome.

Much of the Corfiot terrain is rocky and uneven and walking boots or strong laced shoes worn with socks are advisable. These also serve as protection against the sand viper whose bite is very poisonous. Insect bites and stings can be a problem in summer and it is a good idea to carry a repellent and an anti-histamine cream.

Far outweighing these possible annoyances is the opportunity to observe the rich bird life and to marvel at the profusion of wild flowers.

The Corfu Book of Walks, obtainable on the island, suggests itineraries and draws attention to the flowers, birds and reptiles; *Landscapes of Corfu* by Noel Rochford also details some excellent walks, several of which are quite

Windsurfing, west coast

strenuous. For the energetic scrambler the peaks of Mount Pantokrator and Agii Deka offer a stiff challenge and the reward of magnificent views.

Every summer, areas of scorched trees and 'maquis' scar the island. It is imperative to be extremely careful when extinguishing a cigarette, and it is forbidden by law to light a fire in the open air between 16 May and 15 October. If you discover a forest fire, ring the emergency tel. no: 191.

WATER-SKIING

The sport may be enjoyed or learned at almost every resort. Tuition is available at Kommeno Bay, Dasia, Pyrgi, Nissaki, Glifada, Messongi, Benitses and Perama, among others.

WINDSURFING

Windsurfing can be practised from all the principal beaches and tuition is on offer at many of them. As the prevailing summer wind is from the north-west, the beaches of western Corfu afford the most exciting conditions, especially in the afternoons when it blows most strongly. Beginners may prefer to perfect the skill on the quieter eastern coast: Dino's Ski Club at Pyrgi will give expert instruction.

Excursions

COACH EXCURSIONS

Many visitors to Corfu are under the care of a holiday representative whose company will offer a variety of coach trips. It is in fact very easy for the independent traveller to join such a tour by enquiring at one of the many local travel agents. The selection of excursions offered in Corfu Town will include a 'tour of the island' which usually weaves around the capital, proceeding to Kanoni for the famous view of 'Mouse Island' and thence to Gastouri and the Achilleion (see pp.158–9). The coach then crosses the island to Paleokastritsa, before climbing up to Lakones for the 'aerial' view of the bay. In summer 1990 this day cost 4800 dr. including entrance fees and lunch.

A 'mountain tour' describes a circle around Mount Pantokrator, taking in Strinilas, Acharavi, Kassiopi and Nissaki (price 3800 dr.)

Two evening excursions are popular: 'sunset at Pelekas', seen from the 'Kaiser's throne', followed by a meal at the Taverna Tripa in Kinopiastes (see p.32) – the price of 4200 dr. includes ouzo, food and wine; and the 'Greek night' at Danilia Village which, in 1990, cost 4800 dr. including dinner and wine.

Coach trips from Corfu Town are also advertised to Sidari, Glyfada, Kavos and the Mavromatis distillery (see p.106); each resort is likely to have its own programme of outings.

DANILIA VILLAGE

All over the island this attraction is advertised on hoardings as 'The Corfu Experience'. Follow the Paleokastritsa road 9km north from Corfu Town and turn left at Gouvia; brown and white signs lead the way through the lanes. Danilia is a life-size model of a Corfiot village incorporating all the vernacular architecture of the island, and has a genuinely rural setting. Passing an old olive press at the entrance, a cobbled street lined with a dozen colonnaded shops and two or three restaurants leads to the central square and the church of Agia Irini with its classic bell tower.

The folk museum is divided into rooms fully furnished with artefacts, some of which are centuries old and all claiming to be indigenous to Corfu. Among the exhibits are a fifteenth-century wine press, a hand loom, old farm implements, household utensils and a collection of hand-crafted silver and glassware.

All the shops sell a selection of items made by traditional methods: the range includes wild flower perfumes, olive wood objects, silverware, ceramics, jewellery, wall-hangings and hand-loomed carpets.

A *kafeneion* overlooks the square as does a large area of outdoor seating with attendant barbecue. In summer this venue is the setting for dinner *al fresco* at 20.30 for many coachloads of people. The price charged includes unlimited wine, an opportunity to dance and a floor show featuring Greek music, songs and dances. It is usual, and almost certainly more fun, to attend this evening as part of a group rather than turning up independently. All tourist offices and holiday representatives have details.

Although, as a conception, Danilia is a 'mini-Disneyworld' it is totally Greek and was built over a 9-year period by a local family, opening to the public in 1977. It claims to be 'a microcosm of Corfiot life through the ages' and goes some way to achieving this.

Danilia Village is open Monday – Saturday from 10.00–13.00 and 18.00–24.00. (tel: 91621/2 or 36833).

BOAT EXCURSIONS

Within living memory the only easy way to reach the east coast villages from Corfu Town was by boat. A plethora of pleasure craft perpetuates the tradition, plying between the beaches and connecting the capital with all the resorts from Kassiopi in the north to Kavos in the south.

Vidos Island in Corfu harbour, site of a former fortress and prison, is a popular venue for weekend picnics, and caïques leave hourly from the Old Port, taking only 15 minutes for the crossing.

Lazaretto Island in Gouvia bay can be reached from Kommeno Bay, Kontokali and Gouvia; from Perama and Kanoni there are boats to Pontikonissi (Mouse Island).

At Paleokastritsa a water taxi operates a shuttle service between the beaches, to Mirtiotissa and to Liapades for its 'Blue Grotto'. The trimaran *Kalypso Star*, with glass panelled hulls giving a view of the sea bed, circumnavigates 'Odysseus' Rock' (see p.151) approximately every 45 minutes during the day (price 1500 dr. – children half-price) and in the evening at 22.00 hours (price 2000 dr.). Not only do the passengers see the natural undersea world: divers demonstrate 'exploring a shipwreck' and 'retrieving a submerged statue' to the accompaniment of atmospheric music and dramatic lighting effects.

A number of cruises around the island use a large sailing vessel, the *Romantica*. Its programme includes daytime 'fish picnics' and a moonlight sail along the east coast which includes a buffet, wine and live music. This is organised by Charitos Travel (tel: 44611 between 08.00 and 22.00) and

Excursion boat disembarking passengers at a secluded north-eastern beach

costs around 5000 dr. *Romantica* also goes to Paxos, Antipaxos, Mourtos and Parga.

Perhaps the most patronised day excursion is the trip to Paxos and Antipaxos (see below). The venerable ferry, *Kamelia*, is slow but has an old world dignity; the comfortable M.V. *Rena S/11* (inexplicably nicknamed 'Love Boat') sometimes includes Parga in its itinerary (Vassilikis Travel, 13 Xen. Stratigou, tel: 25317 or 40638) as does the larger *City of Piraeus* operated by Cycladic Cruises (46 Xen. Stratigou, tel: 37263 or 37967).

Frequent ferries leave from the Old Port for Igoumenitsa in mainland Greece. Day trips from Kavos include Plataria and Mourtos (see p.103), respectively 12km and 24km south of Igoumenitsa. The offshore north-western islands of Othoni, Erikoussa and Mathraki can be reached from Corfu (Old Port), Sidari and Agios Stefanos (see pp.102–3). International ferries for Brindisi, Bari, Ancona and Dubrovnik sail from the New Port. Tickets for these services are sold by agencies alongside the southern end of the Old Port at the foot of Donzelot St.

Paxos

Paxos, smallest of the seven principal Ionian islands, is 18.5km (or 10 nautical miles) south-east of Corfu and 13km due west of Epirus on the Greek mainland. On all but the haziest of days it is visible from the southern half of Corfu, most clearly from Cape Asprokavos in the extreme south. The island covers an area of less than 30 sq.km and has a permanent population of 1300 which swells to twice that number in summer and is further increased by day trippers from Corfu. There are many excursions to Paxos as well as a car ferry and a passenger ferry which make the crossing throughout the year. Boat trips leave from Corfu Town, Kavos and Benitses; some of these include a call at Parga in Epirus but, if so, only allow two hours on Paxos. Some offer a short additional stop at Antipaxos.

Like Corfu, Paxos is an island of green forests and white limestone crags. Almost at its geographical centre, the church of Agios Charalambos crowns the highest point at 250m. Hundreds of thousands of mature olive trees grow on terraced hillsides and the olive oil is some of the best in Greece. Disused presses and collapsing windmills are reminders of the relatively recent introduction of mechanisation and electricity. The many stone bridges indicate a network of streams which dry up in summer: there is an annual water shortage following the influx of the holidaymakers.

No classical ruins remain despite the island having been

known to the Ancient Greeks. The island community was converted to Christianity by Gaius, a disciple of St Paul who is the addressee of the apostle's third epistle. Gaios, the capital of Paxos, was named after him.

A 'main road' describes a circle around Paxos but only touches the coast at Lakka, Loggos and Gaios. All three of these fishing ports are at the heads of sheltered inlets and are perfect havens for yachts. Gaios, the main harbour and centre of population, is on the eastern side. Its picturesque streets are narrow and the quay is well served by tavernas and bars; the conspicuous four-storey building on the waterfront is the former British Resident's house dating from the nineteenth-century occupation of Corfu. A ruined Venetian fort on the island of Agios Nikolaos guards the harbour, while a lighthouse stands on the smaller islet of Panagia. Just 1 km south of Gaios is the Paxos Beach Hotel, the only hotel on the island, but there are villas, apartments and rooms to let all over Paxos.

Lakka is the 'second' port of Paxos and its most northerly. Facing north over a shallow bay, it has a fine Byzantine church, low houses painted in unconventional shades and a beach of white pebbles. Loggos, between Lakka and Gaios on the east coast, is perhaps the prettiest of the three villages.

Three or four buses a day link the main settlements and will stop anywhere on request. Bicycles, mopeds and motorcycles are available for hire. Car hire can only be arranged from Corfu; an easier option is to negotiate a tour in a local taxi, whose prices are usually reasonable.

Paxos is ideal for walking, as there are many tracks and paths. This is without doubt the best way to appreciate the abundant wild flowers and birds in spring and autumn. Noel Rochford's book *Landscapes of Paxos* describes many delightful walks.

The island lends itself to exploration by boat as many of its coves and beaches are inaccessible or difficult to reach from land. This is particularly true of the western coast where the cliffs are very high, sheer and honeycombed with caves. As well as being a paradise for divers and snorkellers, these are the haunts of monk seals and dolphins. Of the large caves, Ortholithos is the most visited and is identifiable by an impressive monolithic limestone stack at the entrance; small boats can penetrate about 5m inside the cavern. Further north is the lofty cave of Kastanitha whose roof is 185m high; and, near Lakka, the grotto of Ipapanti. The water around the western seaboard is exceptionally clear and deep. Boat trips around the island take about 90 minutes and ply from Gaios and Corfu.

In the far south, the sandy beach on the islet of Moggonissi is always crowded in summer as all the other accessible beaches are of shingle. A regular boat service runs between Gaios and Moggonissi where there is windsurfing and a taverna.

Antipaxos

Only two nautical miles from the southerly tip of Paxos lies Antipaxos; the strait can be crossed by small boat in 15 minutes. It is more usual, however, to arrive from Gaios: caiques ply to and fro during the summer, taking around 30 to 40 minutes from Gaios to Vrikes beach.

Antipaxos is a tiny island, only 3 sq.km, and supports a permanent population of less than forty, all of whom live on the eastern side. Conditions for these residents are easier since electricity arrived but there is an acute water shortage in summer. The western coast has precipitous cliffs, as high as those on Paxos, but in the east the land slopes gently to exquisite sandy bays and the small harbour of Agrapidia. Both Vrikes and Voutoumi have sparklingly clear water; the former has a beach of white sand incomparable in the Ionian, and the latter, equally white but with some pebbles, is unrivalled as a beauty spot. From June to September a taverna opens at Vrikes and a beach bar is set up at Voutoumi. There is no obvious tourist accommodation on Antipaxos but a few simple villas may be rentable: enquire on Paxos.

The interior of the island is covered with vineyards intersected with neat cobbled paths. The vines are tended by growers from Paxos and produce a semi-sparkling rosé wine which is fairly prestigious in the Ionian; it is sold in Gaios and in Corfu Town.

The North-Western Islands

These three small islands are the most westerly outposts of Greece. The largest, Othoni, is nearly 20km from Sidari and 60km from Corfu Town: it covers an area of about 10 sq.km and is perhaps the most picturesque of the three. Densely forested with olive and pine trees, it has many small sandy bays, particularly on its southern coast, and a prominent mediaeval fortress. Most of the 400 inhabitants are engaged in fishing or olive and vine cultivation. Nearer Sidari are two smaller islets, Mathraki at 8km and Erikoussa at 9km. Both are populated, have two villages each, grow olives and depend on fishing. A small hotel on Erikoussa, named after the island, has 38 rooms (tel: 0663-31457) and some simple accommodation is available on Mathraki.

A ferry operates to all three islands from Corfu Old Port

The fortress of Angelokastro

Cave chapel of Agios Kyriaki at Angelokastro   (below) One
of the abandoned churches of Old Perithia

Evening at Agios Gordis

Agios Georgiou Bay and Cape Arilla

and day trips by motorboat can be joined at Kassiopi, Roda and Sidari. In high season there is a boat from Agios Stefanos, south-west of Sidari, to Mathraki.

The Greek Mainland

Parga is much patronised by boats from Corfu and Paxos, and is an historic and picturesque small town with steep streets, built like an amphitheatre overlooking a glorious bay. A Venetian castle surmounts the northerly headland and the pretty island of Panagia is crowned by a church. Olive, orange and lemon trees crowd the hillsides and several sandy beaches offer good swimming. *City of Piraeus* passengers are given the option of a coach excursion south to Nekromandio, the temple of the Oracle of the Dead alongside the River Acheron, one of the rivers of Hades in mythology.

Other excursions can be made to **Plataria**, a small fishing village with a long shingly beach, and **Mourtos** (Sivota), a pretty fishing harbour and small beach.

For the dedicated 'island-hopper': a 24-hour trip may be made every other day from the New Port at Corfu Town and can be arranged by a local travel agent. *Ionis*, a regular ferry, leaves Corfu at 06.45 for Patras in the Peloponnese, making 45-minute calls at Igoumenitsa (on the mainland), Paxos, Ithaca and Cefalonia before reaching its destination in the early evening. The return journey is overnight, leaving Patras at 22.00 and arriving back in Corfu at 06.00 the next day.

Albania

Since 1987 it has been possible for UK nationals to arrange a visit to Albania from Corfu although this does require some forward planning. Five days prior to the trip, which only goes on a Saturday, it is necessary to apply for a visa and to pay the sum of £33 (in 1990). The day trip cost 5000 dr. in summer 1990 and is bookable through Philmar Travel at 16 Kapodistriou St. Departure from Corfu Town is at 09.00 and arrival at Saranda is 90 minutes later. A luxury air-conditioned coach meets the boat and takes the passengers to neighbouring archaeological sites followed by a sumptuous four or five course lunch in an hotel: this is included in the price of the excursion. Arrival back in Corfu is at 18.30.

The situation in Albania and its relations with other countries may, of course, have changed prior to the publication of this book.

Shopping

Corfu Town is the shopper's mecca and offers an exciting range of goods, many of which make admirable souvenirs.

Domestic shopping is often most conveniently achieved in a supermarket, of which there are plenty. A bottle of local **olive oil** or a jar of **olives** is a very appropriate souvenir and is bought most cheaply from one of these. Freshly made and often delicious food is to be found in small specialist shops. The Corfiots enjoy *patisserie* and the window displays are enticing. Greek nougat (*mandolato*) is sold attractively boxed, as is *loukoumi* (Turkish Delight).

A bustling market is held in Dessila St, at the base of the New Fort: it is open until 13.30 each day. Corfu's fruit and vegetables are sold here, alongside produce from elsewhere in Greece. There are also stalls selling fish, local cheese, honey and live chickens.

Souvenir shops in the town are almost always open throughout the day until late evening, except on Sundays. Apart from these, most shops open from 08.00 to 14.00 on Mondays, Wednesdays and Saturdays; from 08.00 to 13.00 and 17.00 to 20.00 on Tuesdays, Thursdays and Fridays. The main concentration of gift shops is in the area behind the Liston, in N. Theotiki, Spiridonos and Filellinon Sts. Here are rows of small retail outlets, whose wares spill out on to the street and are displayed on their outside walls. You will be tempted by cascades of **sponges** in all sizes (although not all of high quality); cassettes of **Greek music**;

Sponges for sale in Corfu Town

straw hats and baskets; dolls in national costume; *komboloi* (worry beads); onyx ornaments from the mainland; goatskin rugs; woven shoulder bags from Epirus; embroidered cotton tablecloths, shawls and bedspreads; and art shops selling colourful island scenes.

Several shops specialise in items made of olive wood, sometimes worked on the premises. These are expertly crafted and carved. Olive wood to be used in this way is stored for four years while it dries. At the end of this period only 10 per cent of the wood will be suitable for use. This can mean that no large items such as fruit bowls can be carved from a particular branch but the craftsman uses the good wood for fashioning small objects: of these, the miniature fruits and acorns are quite exquisite.

Both gold and silver are cheaper in Greece than in the UK and the making of jewellery has been a local speciality since classical times. Geometric Minoan motifs and representations of dolphins or fish remain popular designs. The Byzantine era saw the introduction of fine gold filigree and the use of coloured precious stones: the jewellers of Evg. Voulgareos St and its environs are well stocked with engagement and dress rings of high quality. Silversmithing arrived with the Venetians; today Paleologou St prides itself on its workshops, where the metal is worked as in Venetian times.

Corfu Town has a large selection of shops selling leather and furs. Traditionally the Mandouki area, which is now known for its fish restaurants and discos, was important for its leather factories. The skins are now prepared on the mainland and the factories have moved out of town: a large factory and sales outlet can be visited at Alepou and another lies almost opposite the Mavromatis distillery on the road to Paleokastritsa. Slightly higher prices can be expected in the town shops, but some will make articles to the customer's size and design: clothes, shoes, handbags or belts.

Many of the fashion items in the high class boutiques on Ag. Panton and Kapidistriou Sts are designed in Corfu and are refreshingly original with moderate price tags. A four-storey department store, Europa, is to be found at 100 Evg. Voulgareos St.

Some keenly priced knitwear is for sale on the island: the Corfu Knitting Factory has outlets in Kontokali and Dasia which are open daily from 09.00 to 14.30 and 17.00 to 23.00. In the capital, the Woolhouse at 31 I. Theotiki sells handmade woollens and will take orders.

In Filellinon St a fascinating shop claims to stock 200 different chess pieces made in wood, bronze and onyx.

Ceramics, made either in Corfu or on the mainland, are

an attractive purchase. Various dealers operate in the gift shop area, some claiming to charge 'factory prices'. Two workshops with a good range of pots stand alongside the main road between Gouvia and Sgombou and there is a further factory shop at Alepou.

An excellent **bookshop** is worth seeking out: Lycoudis at 65 Evg. Voulgareos St has a large selection, including a good range of maps; also some English titles.

Perhaps one of the most visited 'out of town' shops is Mavromatis, the Corfu Distillery, located 13 km from the capital on the Paleokastritsa road. From April to October it is open from 09.00 to 20.00 (10.00 to 15.00 for groups). Their speciality is **koumkouat** liqueur and its derivatives: it comes in sweet, dry, red, orange and green versions. You will be encouraged to avail yourself of copious free samples: be careful if you are driving. Boxes of crystallised *koumkouats* are also on sale. Various brands of *ouzo* are sold here, also the cheap but acceptable Britannia Club gin, some good Greek **brandy** and a range of Corfiot **wines** (tel: 0663-22174/22504).

Finally, a trip to Kassiopi provides the opportunity to visit Aleka's Lace House at the extreme eastern end of the harbour. Aleka Vlachou's shop is open Monday to Saturday from 08.30 to 23.00 and bears the legend 'handmade lace – we keep the tradition for you'. Inside, the old looms are on display and **lace goods** at prices from 400 dr. upwards crowd the small shop: handkerchieves, aprons, pillowcases, tablecloths and bedspreads are all made on the premises and lengths of lace may also be bought. Aleka has framed newspaper cuttings to prove the patronage of Princess Margaret among her many customers.

Distillery showroom, Paleokastritsa road

CLOTHING SIZES

Shoes

Men – British	7	8	9	10	10½	11
American	7½	8½	9½	10½	11	11½
Continental	40	41	42	43	44	45½
Women-British	3	4	5	6	7	8
American	4½	5½	6½	7½	8½	9½
Continental	36	37	38	39	40	41

Shirts (men's)

British and US	14	15	16	17	18
Continental	36	38	41	43	45

Women's dresses

British	10	12	14	16	18	20
American	8	10	12	14	16	18
Continental	40	42	44	46	48	50

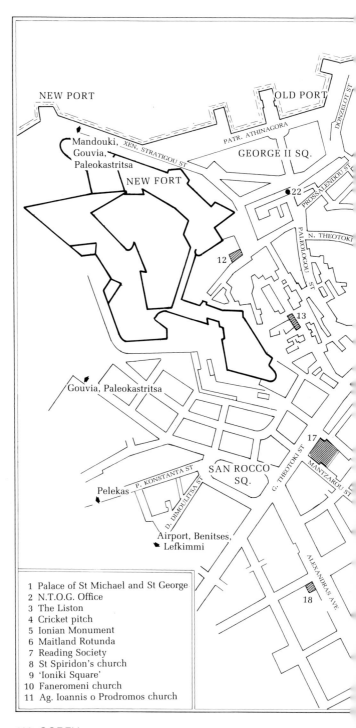

NEW PORT

OLD PORT

Mandouki, Gouvia, Paleokastritsa

XEN. STRATIGOU ST

PATR. ATHINAGORA

GEORGE II SQ.

NEW FORT

22

N. THEOTOKI

PROSSALENDOU ST

PALEOLOGOU ST

DONZELOT ST

12

13

Gouvia, Paleokastritsa

17

MANTZAROU ST

SAN ROCCO SQ.

G. THEOTOKI ST

Pelekas

P. KONSTANTA ST

D. DIMOULITSA ST

Airport, Benitses, Lefkimmi

ALEXANDRAS AVE.

18

1 Palace of St Michael and St George
2 N.T.O.G. Office
3 The Liston
4 Cricket pitch
5 Ionian Monument
6 Maitland Rotunda
7 Reading Society
8 St Spiridon's church
9 'Ioniki Square'
10 Faneromeni church
11 Ag. Ioannis o Prodromos church

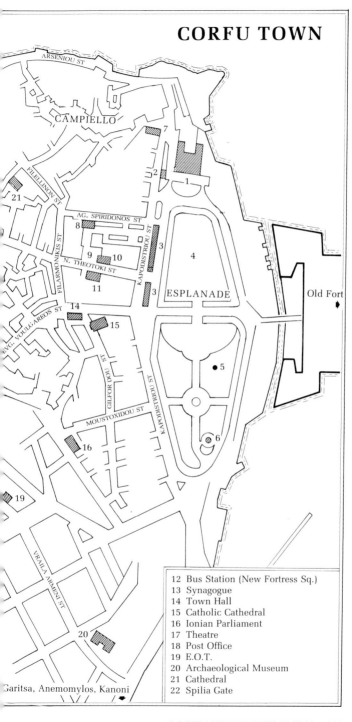

CORFU TOWN

ARSENIOU ST

CAMPIELLO

FIL.ELLINON ST

FILARMONIKIS ST

AG. SPIRIDONOS ST

N. THEOTOKI ST

KAPODISTRIOU ST

EVG. VOULGAREOS ST

ESPLANADE

Old Fort

GILFOR DOU ST

MOUSTOXIDOU ST

KAPODISTRIOU ST

VRAILA ARMENI ST

Garitsa, Anemomylos, Kanoni

12 Bus Station (New Fortress Sq.)
13 Synagogue
14 Town Hall
15 Catholic Cathedral
16 Ionian Parliament
17 Theatre
18 Post Office
19 E.O.T.
20 Archaeological Museum
21 Cathedral
22 Spilia Gate

CORFU TOWN (KERKYRA)

Corfu Town is one of the most appealing provincial cities in the Mediterranean. The architecture is largely Venetian, and despite the bombardments suffered during the Second World War, large sections of the town have been well preserved. The natural beauty of the site, the proximity of the sea and the elegance of the buildings, together with the relaxed lifestyle of its inhabitants, combine to produce a city to be enjoyed.

Corfu Town is full of picturesque corners, of flowers (in baskets or sprouting from mellowed walls), of music, unexpected ancient wells and slanting sunlight. The houses in the old parts of the town are tall and huddled together above narrow flagged streets – for centuries Corfu was hemmed in by its defensive walls and the only direction in which it could expand was upwards – but the proximity of the sea on three sides keeps the town cool and airy even in the hottest months. For the visitor, one of the greatest pleasures is the absence of traffic: except for the Esplanade and the road around the sea wall, few of the old town's streets are accessible by car: while in the narrow alleys (*kandounia*) and steps of the Campiello scooter-powered light trucks have to be used for most deliveries.

The classical city was built on the Kanoni peninsula (see p.65) but moved to the site of the present Old Fort after the fall of the Roman Empire for the additional protection it afforded from barbarian raiding parties. On this tiny peninsula, named Korypho after its two peaks (*koruphai* in Byzantine Greek) and increasingly fortified down the centuries, the townspeople huddled, until under the Venetians increasing prosperity compelled the population to overflow and work began on the New Fort (in 1570), with formidable walls enclosing the area between the two. Later occupiers of Corfu also left their mark on the city: the French with the elegant Parisian arcades of the Liston, the British with the confidently imperialistic neoclassicism of the Palace of St Michael and St George, but the Venetian influence remains predominant in the old town. Their walls were not demolished until the nineteenth century – today only two of the four gates through the walls survive (the Spilia Gate onto the Port and the St Nicholas Gate to the sea); the more spacious new parts of the city, Garitsa, San

Gateway, New Fortress: the Venetians transformed Corfu into one of the most strongly defended cities in the Mediterranean

Rocco and Mandouki, all originally outlying villages, are quite different in architecture and atmosphere.

To tour the city, it is sensible to park your car in the Old Port area, near New Fortress Square, where most buses from elsewhere on the island arrive. Brooding over the port stands the powerful bulk of the sixteenth-century **Neon Frourion** (New Fortress). One of the sights of the Mediterranean when it was built, it is said to conceal a maze of passageways and tunnels linking with the Old Fort on its peninsula (during the Second War both forts were used as air raid shelters). Today it is used by the Greek Navy and there is no public access, though one can walk around the walls (and through a tunnel which penetrates the eastern arm of the fortifications, between the bus station and the lively vegetable market held in what was once the moat), to admire the Venetian lions which adorn the gateways and some of the walls.

Walk through George II Square (Plateia Georgiou B'), a large open space fronting the ferry port, which is ablaze with the pink blossom of Judas trees in spring. In the centre colourful horse-drawn cabs wait for customers opposite the Spilia gate. At the far end the road climbs onto the sea wall, known as the Mourayia in Venetian times, but Donzelot St today, becoming Arseniou St as it leaves the port, with views of the little island of **Vidos** offshore.

Vidos has a chequered history. The private hunting ground of the Venetian Count Malpiero, it was occupied by the Turks in 1537, who set up a battery and bombarded the Old Fort from the island; in the event, hunger and disease forced them to retreat when the Corfiots were on the point of surrender. In 1716 another invading Turkish army used the same tactic, as did the combined Russian-Turkish fleet which compelled the French to surrender Corfu in 1799 – after this last episode the forests which had previously clothed the island never fully recovered. Its fortifications were dismantled by the British, and the island became a penal settlement and then a cemetery for many of the exiled Serbians who fled to Corfu during World War I. Today Vidos is once again a peaceful beauty spot, which can be visited from the Old Port in Corfu.

Arseniou St continues past offices offering excursions and tourist information, some housed in lofty buildings displaying a worn winged Venetian lion over their doors. One of them, next door to the National Bank, was let to the painter and nonsense versifier Edward Lear during one of his many visits to the island. Another houses the **Solomos Museum** (see p.86), in the building occupied by Greece's national poet Dionysos Solomos from 1828 until his death. Beyond the Solomos Museum, a broad flight of steps leads to the church of **Antivouniotissa**, home of the Byzantine Museum (closed for restoration, see p.85). A number of popular restaurants enjoy the benefit of the spectacular view from the sea wall.

Rounding the corner past the Metropolitan's Palace brings the first sight of the Old Fort on the twin peaks that gave Corfu its name. To the left is the ramp leading down to the sixteenth-century sea **gate of St Nicholas**. Today there is a small lido at the bottom, and a restaurant beside the disused church. The walk continues, passing the elegant frontages of the Old Prefecture with its five laurel wreaths (a previous building on this site was the birthplace of the great John Kapodistrias, first President of Greece), and one of the

The Corfu Literary Society, housing an important collection of old maps and documents

gems of the town – the pretty, apricot-coloured building of the Corfu Reading Society, with its exterior stairs and its graceful loggia, where what survives of the city's archives are stored. We now approach the rear of the **Palace of St Michael and St George**.

Built between 1819 and 1823 as the British Lord High Commissioner's residence (incorporating the Ionian Parliament *and* the Treasury of the Order of St Michael and St George), the building is constructed of limestone imported (like the masons) from Malta to a design by the British architect Sir George Whitmore, R.E. The neoclassical façade, with Doric colonnades and triumphal arches, is well-proportioned and succeeds in blending surprisingly well with the general tone of its architectural surroundings: nevertheless it is an imposing building, explicitly asserting the dignified confidence of the occupying colonial power. After the departure of the British (when a statue of Britannia which once crowned the frontage was removed with much rejoicing), the building passed to the Greek Royal Family until 1913. Today the staterooms may be visited and the Palace also houses the remarkable collections of the Museum of Asian Art (see pp.84–5). In the pavilion at the end of the west wing are the Tourist Office and the headquarters of the Tourist Police.

On the façade of the Palace a frieze represents the emblems of the Ionian islands, while the gardens in front of the building incorporate a lily pond in which stands a bronze statue of Sir Frederick Adam, somewhat bizarrely attired in a Roman toga. Corfu's second British High Commissioner, who married a Corfiot woman and built the villa Mon Repos, he is fondly remembered in the island, particularly for ordering the construction of a system of aqueducts to supply Corfu town with water.

The Esplanade (or Spianada or Plateia) – one of the biggest squares in Europe and the focus of Corfiot life – is now before you, a wide expanse of grass, flowering Judas trees and gardens; as well as incorporating a bandstand, a children's playground and a clutch of statues and monuments, the Esplanade is the site of Corfu's cricket pitch, an incongruous tarmac strip which is covered with coconut matting for matches. All this open space was originally created, quite simply, to provide a clear field of fire from the Fort. In Venetian times it was used for jousting and fairs – there were rainwater cisterns underneath. The British used it as a parade ground.

Proceeding towards the Old Fort, you pass the tiny church of Agios Pandeleimon, known as the 'Mandrakina' because it overlooks the small harbour on the north side of the Old Fort (the Mandraki), where the Venetians' war galleys were moored – some of the mooring posts are still visible. Nearby is a small park containing a statue of the eccentric philhellene Frederick North, Fifth Earl of Guilford (1769–1828), in Greek dress by the Corfiot artist Prosalendis: Guilford was much loved on the island for his adoption of the Orthodox faith and above all for founding the Ionian Academy, the first seat of higher education in modern Greece, to which he donated his considerable library (see p.73). (One of Corfu Town's few public WCs is nearby.)

The entrance to the **Old Fort** is guarded, appropriately, by a more heroic statue. that of Count John Matthias de Schulenberg, the German mercenary in Venetian employ who successfully fought off the Turkish attack in 1716. Beyond lies the bridge which gives access to the Old Fort over the narrow defensive canal dug by the Venetians.

This promontory has probably been fortified to some degree since the seventh or eighth century. The eastern peak was fortified by the Byzantine authorities after a disastrous Ostrogothic raid, and the western in the thirteenth century by the Venetians, who constantly strengthened the Fort's defences over four centuries. The Venetians' centre of government was here, but their official buildings were demolished by the British, who replaced them with barracks and a military hospital which continued in use after their departure. Not until 1979 did the Greek army hand the fort over to the Greek Archaeological Service, who have been working on restoring it ever since. Today an air of dereliction hangs over the Old Fort, and it is hard to imagine its crowded and eventful past.

The Old Fort is open from 08.00–19.00 daily and entrance is free. Entering under a massive vaulted gateway (which may once have been embellished by a magnificent gilded lion now in the Tower of London), a turning to the left leads to the site of the nightly Sound and Light show (see p.34). Round the bend to the right you are confronted by an unexpected sight: a 'Doric temple' which is in fact the garrison church of St George, built by the British in 1840, bombed in 1943–44, restored subsequently but now again in poor repair, with broken windows and roof tiles. A paved path climbs the hillside, passing a Venetian cistern and a clocktower. At the time of writing it is unfortunately not permitted to climb further – a great shame, since the terrace by the Castel Nuovo lighthouse at the top offers a memorable view of Corfu Town, which gives a vivid idea of the way the old town was laid out: if you are able to ascend this far, notice how the streets into the Esplanade radiate in such a way that the Fort's cannon could fire straight down them. There are magnificent views, too, of Mt Pantokrator to the north, while to the south the Kanoni peninsula, the mountains of Agii Deka beyond and the whole curve of the east coast can be seen as far as Cape Lefkimmi.

Leaving the Old Fort, cross over to the Esplanade, veering left a little for a look at the Ionian Monument, placed here to commemorate the unification (*enosis*) of the islands with Greece in 1864, but today unfortunately somewhat marred by graffiti: it bears marble reliefs representing the symbols of the seven islands. South of it is the quaintly Victorian bandstand (where regular concerts are given in summer) and further on the **Maitland Rotunda**, erected in 1816 in tribute to Sir Thomas Maitland ('King Tom'), the first British Lord High Commissioner. Further south still, on the other side of the road, stands the statue of Maitland's harshest critic, John Kapodistrias. The northern half of the Esplanade is bordered by Corfu's celebrated **Liston**, the elegantly proportioned arcade which has been the town's most popular meeting place ever since the French built it in 1807 in emulation of the Rue de Rivoli in Paris. The name originates from the 'List' of noble families, whose members once enjoyed the exclusive right to promenade here. Today the cafés and bars whose tables fill the arcades and spill out into the shade of the acacia trees on the other side of the road provide the perfect setting for a rendezvous over a drink in the morning, at lunchtime, or best of all in the long Corfiot evening when fascinating hours can be spent over an ouzo while watching the endless

The Liston, rendezvous and hub of Corfu's social life

volta going on in the traffic-free street in front. This additional Venetian legacy brings everyone – old men, the trendy young and prosperous families with impossibly smartly dressed children – out into the streets on any fine evening, to stroll and chatter, to see and be seen.

After a drink on the Liston penetrate a block into town and walk along **Kapodistriou St**, which runs behind the Liston to terminate at the southern end of the Esplanade. Here are many fine houses, most of them built by the aristocracy; at the far end stands the burnt-out shell of the Ionian Academy, originally the Grimani barracks, which was destroyed by bombs in 1943 – the Academy once contained Lord Guilford's library and many other priceless manuscripts. Two doors down, the nineteenth-century Cavalieri Hotel with its massive balconies was also bombed but has been carefully restored. Another appealing building is No. 10, decorated by a cartouche of a Corcyraean ship (an inscription tells that this was the house in which Lord Guilford was received into the Orthodox faith), while nos 12 and 14, once the home of the painter Angelos Giallina (1857–1939) share an elegant arcade.

Plunge into town from Kapodistriou St through any of the picturesque, washing-bedecked narrow streets. (Moustoxidou St, named after a celebrated Corfiot historian, is an interesting one to choose: once much wider, and a main thoroughfare in the town, this street was the venue for jousting displays during Carnival – the judges were accommodated on the balcony of the Ricchi mansion, still to be seen above its ornate portico.) All will bring you to Gilfordou (Guilford) St, busy with shoppers. A block further up Moustoxidou St is the Ionian Parliament building, later the Anglican church of the Holy Trinity. Here, on 18 February 1859, Gladstone strove to persuade the members that their interests lay in founding an independent Ionian republic rather than voting for union with the new state of Greece – in vain, as a plaque commemorating the vote for union in 1863 reminds us. This area of Corfu Town was greatly damaged in World War II: of the original Parliament building only the façade remains and around it stand modern blocks of flats.

A right turn down D. Kolla St brings you down to what was the most important square in the old town, Plateia M.

No. 10 Kapodistrias St: the houses of the nobility were scattered evenly throughout the old town

Corfu's Town Hall served as a theatre and opera house for nearly two centuries

Theotoki; at its head, above a bower of bougainvillea, the gracious building now housing the Bank of Greece used to be the Law Courts and before that the palace of the Catholic Archbishop (who took precedence over the Orthodox Metropolitan until the arrival of the British). Lower down stands the decorative Venetian **Town Hall**, one of the most elaborate buildings in the town. Built of white marble from the quarries at Sinies on Mount Pantokrator's eastern slopes, it began life in 1663 as a single-storey loggia and meeting place for the nobility; in 1720 it was converted to become the San Giacomo Theatre and subsequently an opera house before a second storey was added and the building assumed its present civic role in 1903. On the east side is a bust of the Venetian Doge Francesco Morosini, who defeated the Turks in the war of 1684–7 (and was in command on the Athenian Acropolis on the disastrous occasion in 1687 when the Parthenon was blown up by a stray shot from the Turkish forces.) On the east of the square is the Roman Catholic cathedral of St James; severely damaged during the war, it has been restored but the interior holds little of interest except a few fragments of Venetian statuary.

Behind the Town Hall is **Evg. Voulgareos St**, Corfu's 'Bond Street', where silversmiths have worked since Venetian times; to the left, the street terminates where the western gate, the Porto Reale, once stood; a little further north is the old ghetto, centred on Corfu's one remaining synagogue. Beyond the old line of the wall, the broad, modern G. Theotoki St leads to Plateia Georgiou Theotoki (usually known as San Rocco Square), the hub of the modern, traffic-dominated town and the point from which the touring routes around the island commence. San Rocco was once an outlying village, but the square that preserves its name is now surrounded by butchers, ironmongers and other useful if mundane shops (including one of the best supermarkets in town); often choked with traffic, it could be in almost any Greek town.

To continue exploring the old town, however, cross Evg. Voulgareos St behind the Town Hall into M Theotoki St, passing a small market square off which leads Ag. Basileiou St, the street of the fishmongers. **Nikiforou Theotoki St**, reached next, is another major artery of the old town: to the left is an arcaded section, the part of it below the Hotel Crete embellished with a row of vigorously carved heads (known locally as 'the Moors'). To the right, N. Theotoki leads past the gracious white square properly known as Plateia Iroon Kypriakou Agonos ('Square of the Heroes of the Cypriot Struggle'), but commonly referred to as **'Ioniki Square'**

The quiet north-eastern beach at Kaminaki

Sand dunes at Lake Korission

Ancient olive grove, southern Corfu

Cottage in Vatos (below) The sheep are driven home to Vatonies

after the imposing Ionian Bank building (1840) which occupies the western side.

In the centre of the square stands a statue of the Corfiot politician Georgios Theotokis (1843–1916), an early Prime Minister of Greece. (By now the visitor will be becoming accustomed to the ubiquitous presence of this large and influential family! Arriving in Corfu as refugees after the fall of Constantinople in 1453, the Theotikis flourished on the island, furnishing their own ship at the battle of Lepanto and going on to produce generations of writers, landowners and statesmen who have played leading roles in Corfiot life ever since.) There are also two important churches in the square. Opposite the Bank, Panagia Ton Xenon ('Our Lady of the Strangers', so called because it was used by exiles from Epirus when the Greek mainland was under Turkish occupation), is more properly known as the **Faneromeni** (1689); the highly decorated, well lit interior glows with icons, gilded wood and polished metal: the numerous paintings and icons in the church include examples by the Cretan painters Contarini, Michael Tzenos, and Emmanuel Tzanes, with a ceiling painted by the Zakynthiot priest Nicholas Koutouzis in the 18th century.

On the other side of N. Theotoki stands **Agios Ioannis o Prodromos** (St John the Baptist), built in 1520 and for some years Corfu's cathedral. Nikiforos Theotokis (1736–1805), the celebrated orthodox preacher after whom this street is named, was the priest here for many years: his sermons were so popular that the pulpit had to be moved so that he could be heard outside his crowded church – he later became an archbishop in Russia. There is a painted wooden ceiling, a fine portrait of St Demetrios by Tzanes and on the iconostasis is a series of scenes from the life of St John by Tzenos. In the porch the fresco on the left may have been painted by another Cretan, Michael Damaskinos (1535–91), the teacher of El Greco.

A little to the north looms the tallest belfry on the island, that of Corfu Town's most loved church, **Saint Spiridon's**. Built in 1590, the church's chief *raison d'être* is to house the mummified body of Saint Spiridon (see pp.86–7), whom the faithful visit frequently to pay their respects: the casket containing his shrivelled remains lies in the chapel to the right of the altar – except on his procession days, 11 August, Palm Sunday, Easter Saturday and the first Sunday in November, when the Saint is removed and paraded through the streets in a gem-studded reliquary of gilt ebony with a glass panel through which his face can be seen (looking, the late Lawrence Durrell thought, 'a grim little figure, not unlike General Montgomery'). The silver oil lamps are a

Corfu shopping street: confined by its walls, old Corfu was forced to grow upwards around narrow streets

feature of the church and many were donated by the Venetians in their relief at the repulse of the Turks in 1716.

Emerging from the reverent atmosphere of Saint Spiridon's it may come as a shock to be confronted by the offensive T-shirts on sale in the tourist shops of Ag. Spirodonos St, an otherwise typically Venetian thoroughfare. Here turn left, then right into Filarmonikis St, then left again into narrow Filellinon St, which is full of enticements for shoppers. To your right now is the **Campiello**, once regarded as the choicest part of town and still today a delightful largely residential area of tall houses and stepped alleys that is full of fascination (and easy to get temporarily lost in). At the far end of Filellinon St turn right into Ag. Theodoras and climb a short flight of steps to the left a little way up: this brings you to delightful Kremasti Square, with the church of the Presentation of the Virgin on one side: the building is much damaged by damp, and swallows nest in the roof, but an imposing marble iconostasis and some intriguing tomb-stones set in the floor remain unscathed. The square is noted for its beautiful Venetian wellhead, dated 1699, and also for being the home of one of Corfu Town's few outstanding restaurants (open evenings only).

Returning down Ag. Theodoras brings you to Corfu Town's Orthodox **cathedral**, fronted by a broad flight of steps. The church, which became the cathedral only in 1841, is dedicated to St Theodora, and her remains are preserved here. Among many fine icons the cathedral contains one outstanding one, that of St George by Damaskinos on a pillar near the main door. From here it is simply a matter of walking down the steps to return to the Old Port: alternatively make your way past the cathedral to find N. Theotoki St again, which connects the Esplanade with the harbour.

THE OUTSKIRTS OF TOWN

Platitera Convent
Reached under an archway off busy Ioulias Andreadi St, the main road from San Rocco Square to Paleokastritsa and the north, the convent offers a haven of calm from the busy traffic outside. Bougainvillea shrouds a courtyard with an ancient well beside which stands the church, first built in 1743 but extensively rebuilt in 1801 after the bombardment of Mandouki by the French: the separate Venetian-style belfry was added later. The church is usually kept dark, but the rich decoration of the interior can just be discerned, with an elaborate iconostasis and a number of fine paintings, many of them by the eighteenth-century artist Koutouzis. Behind the altar lies the simple tomb of John Kapodistrias, first President of Greece. After his assassination the British, fearful of an uprising, buried him here in secrecy.

The British Cemetery
A little way out of town to the west (signposted down a lane going left off the main road to the airport four blocks from San Rocco Square), the cemetery is a peaceful haven with much to interest the botanist. Here lie the bodies of the British officials and troops who died on the island during the Protectorate – a surprisingly large number. The cemetery is

well-maintained and evocative; grassy paths which in spring are studded with wild orchids in profligate variety meander between the graves, the most recent of which are those of the 44 British sailors who died in the second 'Corfu Incident', when their ships sailed into an Albanian minefield in the Corfu channel in 1946. (It was this episode which led to the severing of British relations with Albania, a rift which at the time of writing appeared likely to be healed at last.) South of the cemetery a circular wall encloses the Penitentiary, built by the British on a small hill on which one of Corfu Town's outer fortresses once stood. The prison was once the most modern in Europe, with single cells for each inmate.

Garitsa Bay and Kanoni

The southern outskirts of Corfu Town extend along the shores of Garitsa bay to the suburb of Anemomylos, with the village of Analipsis and the Kanoni peninsula, site of the ancient Corcyra beyond. To visit them either proceed along the water's edge from the southern end of the Esplanade (past the Corfou Palace Hotel and the Archaeological Museum) or follow Alexandras Ave from San Rocco Square; this broad leafy avenue reaches the sea at the monument to Sir Howard Douglas, an energetic builder of roads, prisons, a hospital and a lunatic asylum who was the British Lord High Commissioner from 1835–41. During the British Protectorate Garitsa was the separate village of Castrades and a favourite place for a Victorian promenade with the ladies beside the sea. Much, much earlier the area was the site of the ancient necropolis, and a number of tombs have come to light, most notably the circular memorial to one Menecrates, a foreigner whose memory was honoured about 600 BC for the services he had rendered to Corcyra's interests on the mainland. Today the tomb, under its conical roof, stands in a corner of the rather dreary yard of a wistaria-smothered police station a block inland from the Douglas obelisk.

Follow the road (Mitropolitou Athanassiou St) that leads southwards a block inland until it divides and becomes one-way, and park wherever convenient shortly afterwards. The suburb of Anemomylos lies to your left on land which was once the so-called Alcinous Harbour, one of the twin ports of the ancient city; nowadays there is a shingle beach here, with changing rooms and a snack bar, which for a small fee offers the nearest sea bathing to Corfu Town. Down a side street to the left is the extremely attractive eleventh-century church of **SS Jason and Sosipater**, the only completely authentic Byzantine church on the island (parts of the chapel on Mouse Island and the church of St Stavromenos

Church of SS Jason and Sosipater, Anemomylos

near Nimfes may also date from this period, as may the church of Ag. Merkourios at Agios Markos). Jason and Sosipater were disciples of St Paul and bishops of Iconium and Tarsus respectively, who brought Christianity to Corfu, probably during the reign of Caligula; subsequently martyred (apparently by being burned alive in a bronze bull), their remains were buried in Corfu but later removed by the Angevins. The interior of the church is well lit by windows in the octagonal dome over the typical Byzantine cross-shaped structure. Two magnificent columns of black marble salvaged from some earlier temple separate the vestibule and many of the large blocks which form the walls must also have come from classical buildings in the area; icons include portrayals of the two saints and other works by the Cretan Emmanuel Tzanes, and there are remains of frescoes on some of the walls. The church is open most days from 08.30–20.30.

Continue south and turn right at a T-junction; almost immediately the entrance to the villa of Mon Repos appears on your left. Built in 1824 for the British Commissioner Sir Frederick Adam, the villa was later presented to the Greek Royal family as a summer residence (Prince Philip, Duke of Edinburgh, was born in the house), to whom it still belongs. Today it stands deserted and inaccessible within its luxuriant grounds, beneath which lies much of the commercial area of old Corcyra. Opposite the entrance stand the ruins of the oldest church on Corfu, the fifth-century basilica of **Agia Kerkyra** (also known as Paleopolis church). Built on the site of a series of temples going back to a thousand years earlier, the walls incorporate columns, capitals, lions' heads and numerous other remnants of earlier structures. Over subsequent centuries the church has been rebuilt many times, only to be gutted by a bomb in 1943.

Paleopolis, the name commonly given to this region, means 'Old City', for the walls of ancient Corcyra ran from Anemomylos across the peninsula to the city's other port, known as the Hyllaic harbour, in the Chalikiopoulos lagoon (today spanned by the airport runway). On the opposite side of the road from Agia Kerkyra archaeological excavations are in progress, and a walk down the lane beside the church (signposted 'Stratia') brings you to the Convent of Agios Theodoros with the remains of the large Doric **Temple of Artemis** (from which the Gorgon pediment in the Archaeological Museum was excavated) nearby. Traces of the old city wall survive here, also.

Opposite Agia Kerkyra a road leads uphill to the small village of **Analipsis** (meaning 'Ascension', it is the scene of a notable festival on Ascension Day). This was almost certainly the old acropolis of Corcyra, though due to subsequent reuse of the ancient materials, few traces of its classical past remain today. Significant remains of a sixth-century temple of Apollo have been discovered, but most of them are covered by vegetation in the Mon Repos grounds. It is sometimes possible to discern a glimpse over the walls, however, by taking a path to the left (reached by making as if to enter the Taverna Kardakis) just before the road turns sharply left and peters out at the far end of the village. The path leads sharply downhill beside the wall of Mon Repos to reach the sea; on the way it passes the celebrated **Kardaki Spring**, where water flows still from the mouth of an almost obliterated Venetian lion of great age.

Returning from Analipsis, turn left (following signs to 'Figareto') to continue along the peninsula: the road around it is a single one-way loop. The **Kanoni** ('battery') peninsula, so named from the single cannon placed at the end by the French, has long been noted as a beauty spot: the British, particularly, seem to have regarded a stroll down the peninsula as a regular part of the social timetable – Edward Lear complains in one of his letters that he 'insisted on not pottering to the one-gun battery – which is like walking up and down Rotten Row'. To a large extent this idyllic setting has now been spoilt by a rash of new building: the peninsula boasts a number of hotels (including the Hilton), and expensive villas with lush gardens and is one of the most built-up areas on the island. Yet the tourist buses still arrive in droves. The attraction, of course, is the famous view over the mouth of the lagoon, which is still stunning: in the

The much photographed view from Kanoni, hackneyed but still delightful

foreground lies the 'floating' convent of **Vlacherna** and beyond it the cypresses almost obscure the chapel on **'Mouse Island' (Pontikonissi)**, believed by some to be the petrified shape of the Phaeacian ship turned to stone by Poseidon as it returned from taking Odysseus home to Ithaca.

A restaurant/bar at the end of the peninsula road offers a broad terrace from which to enjoy the view – and sample the remarkable sensation of seeing jet aircraft take off and land right in front of you! The noise is intermittently earsplitting, making the popularity of Kanoni as a residential area somewhat hard to understand; but for a short period the experience of enjoying a drink while looking down onto the runway of an international airport is interestingly different!

Below the viewpoint lies the pedestrian causeway across the lagoon to Perama (see p.169). From this level it is possible to visit the tiny glittering chapel of the Vlacherna convent and, if you are interested, secure the services of a boatman to take you to Pontikonissi, where the pretty little chapel of the Pentokrator may be as old as the eleventh or twelfth century. Round to the left, out of sight of the airport, is Kanoni's man-made beach. From the end of the peninsula the road turns back, returning to Agia Kerkyra and Anemomylos by a slightly higher route.

TOURING CORFU

1: *The North-East*

The landscapes of north-eastern Corfu are among the island's most dramatic. From Pyrgi, at the northern extremity of the 'Corfu Riviera', this route follows the line of the coast: it offers stunning views of the Albanian mountains just across the straits, while on the landward side the scenery is always dominated by the craggy bulk of Mount Pantokrator, the island's highest mountain. At the ancient port of Kassiopi in Corfu's north-east corner the coast becomes less vertiginous, before the route turns inland around Pantokrator's western foothills for a return journey affording panoramic views of much of the island. Diversions along the way can be made to a number of beaches and small fishing villages, to the almost deserted village of Old Perithia on Pantokrator's northern flank, and to the summit of the mountain itself.

From Corfu Town the main road north can be found either by following signs to Paleokastritsa from Plateia Georgiou Theotoki (San Rocco Square), or by taking the waterfront road past the port through the suburb of Mandouki; this brings you to the main northern road at a T-junction shortly afterwards.

Soon after this junction an imposing belfry is visible to the left. This adorns the church of the inland town of **Potamos**, bypassed by the busy main road, which is named after the river which flows into the sea nearby. (The belfry was the subject of a fine watercolour by Edward Lear.) Potamos Bay, to your right, was where the combined Russian and Turkish forces landed at the outset of their successful invasion of Corfu in 1798; it may also have been (as the great archaeologist and excavator of Troy, Schliemann, believed) the site of Nausicaa's discovery of the shipwrecked Odysseus. Today a small satellite resort, **Alikes Potamou** (the name tells us that there were once salt-pans here), has grown up around the main road, with some tourist facilities centred on the Sunset Hotel and the large Kerkyra Golf Hotel – inexplicably named, since there are no golfing facilities anywhere near, though there is a popular horse-riding establishment next door. Alikes Potamou has a thin strip of beach, with very shallow water and, unusually for the east coast of Corfu, soft sand, but is really used only by visitors staying locally and citizens of Corfu Town at weekends; there is access from the main road via a narrow track running along the northern side of the horse-riding centre.

This stretch of road is among the busiest in Corfu and is gradually being widened to form a dual carriageway for much of its length. Immediately after Alikes Potamou, it runs along the water's edge for a brief stretch, with views of Vidos island behind and Lazaretto ahead, before reaching **Kontokali**, the first of a string of beach resorts along this section of the coast, about 6 km from Corfu Town.

Kontokali itself lies on a slip road between the main road and the sea; the village is sited on the neck of the promontory that shelters Gouvia Bay, with views of the offshore island of Lazaretto; it is almost entirely given over to tourism, consisting of a strip of bars, shops and eating places, with a small strip of pebbly beach. The overall effect is of scruffiness and haphazard development: Kontokali represents touristic Corfu at its least attractive and cannot really be said to repay a visit.

The slip road through Kontokali continues, skirting the bay, to reach the next resort, **Gouvia**, almost immediately; here it rejoins the main road. Gouvia Bay is a beautiful natural harbour offering fine views of Mount Pantokrator, and it is easy to see why the area has long been popular with visitors to Corfu. Known as Govino until well into the present century, Gouvia was the landing spot chosen by the troops of the Turkish Sultan Suleiman the Magnificent

The Arsenal, Gouvia, survivor of an era when the village offered a favourite landing spot for invaders

when they invaded Corfu in 1537, and later became an important naval base under the Venetians. Readers of Gerald Durrell's *My Family and Other Animals* will recall that in the 1930s seaplanes used to land here (the 'Daffodil-Yellow Villa', the Durrells' second home on the island, stood on the hills above the bay).

Today Gouvia is a busy resort with a number of hotels and villa complexes and a wide range of eating and drinking establishments. Considerably smarter and more sedate than Kontokali and generally quieter than the resorts to its north, the village has an attractively curving, fairly deep beach of small pebbles becoming larger (and occasionally weed-covered) nearer the sea. It is, however, small and can be crowded. Watersports facilities include waterskiing, parascending, 'sharky' rides, jet skis and a 'hydroslide', with pedaloes and other small boats as well as sunbeds and umbrellas for hire in season. There are beach bars and restaurants close by behind the Molfeta Beach Hotel. Much of the bay front at Gouvia is occupied by an enormous marina; behind it the massive ribs of a ruined Venetian arsenal (shipyard), Gouvia's only reminder of its tempestuous past, still stand in a field of meadow flowers.

The main road continues, having skirted Kontokali and Gouvia (and passed the turning for Danilia Village, see p.98), to head straight for the looming bulk of Mt Pantokrator. Less than 1 km after the Gouvia slip road rejoins the main road, there is an important road junction at Tsavros. Here the Paleokastritsa road carries straight on, but our route turns off to the right, opposite the Tsavros supermarket. The traffic is considerably lighter after the Tsavros junction, as the road leaves Gouvia bay and turns inland across the neck of Cape Kommeno. (A minor route to the right continues round the northern edge of the bay, leading to the prettily sited church of Papandis and a number of hotels on the cape.)

Still heading due north, the road remains a few hundred metres inland as it passes Dafnila Bay and the next major resort, **Dasia**. Built mainly among olive groves between the main road and the sea, Dasia is an extremely popular resort, dominated by two large hotels. Roads and tracks lead from the main road towards the beach, which is a long strip of gently shelving pebble and shingle some 6 m wide, becoming more sandy at the northern end (which is occupied by the Polynesian huts of the Club Méditerranée on a small cypress-covered promontory). Though the beach can become unpleasantly crowded, Dasia is well-treed (the name derives from '*dasos*', meaning 'forest') and benefits from the absence of a road along the beach itself. The resort also enjoys pleasant views of Cape Kommeno, Vidos Island and Corfu Town. As well as hotels and villas, there are numerous tavernas and bars, as well as some shops and discos, among the trees and along the beach. Caique excursions to other parts of the coast operate from several landing stages and there is a full range of watersports. A little to the north lies the peaceful and prosperous village of Kato Korakiana.

About 4 km from the Tsavros junction the sea suddenly reappears and the rugged coast to the north comes into view; the road returns to sea level as it enters the linked settlements of **Ipsos** and **Pyrgi**. These two resorts, unlovely but very popular (particularly with the younger element) consist of a long strip of shops, restaurants, discos and bars; as yet much of the development penetrates only a block or two inland from the road, which separates it from a narrow (and somewhat weedy) beach of small pebbles and coarse sand. The beach shelves gently and becomes markedly sandier at the northern (Pyrgi) end. Watersports are an important feature here, and paragliding is available as well as waterskiing, windsurfing and scuba diving.

Both Ipsos and Pyrgi are almost entirely modern creations. Not many years ago they were tiny offshoot settlements of the village of Agios Markos lying above them on the lower slopes of Pantokrator, whose traditional agricultural lands the resorts now occupy; following a series of alarming landslips at Agios Markos, the island government financed some of the residents to build new houses on the level ground below the village, and it is from these settlements that the modern resorts developed. Traces of old Ipsos and Pyrgi are hard, but not impossible, to find: in the former, for example, a line of half a dozen old cottages at the extreme southern end of the beach remain from a more tranquil past, together with a fine old church behind them.

Particularly in August, both these resorts can be vulgar, garish and noisy, but it is still possible to wander a few hundred metres inland from the tourist strip and come across an old woman on her donkey plodding along a green lane between the olive groves.

After Pyrgi the road climbs steeply up the southern foothills of Pantokrator, and the most scenic part of the route begins. Once a Venetian mule path, it is hard to imagine that this spectacular road was built less than a generation ago – before that all travel in this part of the island had to be accomplished on foot, on horseback or by boat. Before embarking on the drive round the coastal corniche, however, a brief diversion to **Agios Markos** (4 km) may be found rewarding:

As the road climbs from Pyrgi, the turning for Agios Markos is to the left on a hairpin bend; the village, appearing scarcely populated at most times of day during the tourist season, is a delightfully tranquil collection of old houses set on a steep slope at the base of Mt Pantokrator, with fine views of Ipsos Bay and beyond. Steep steps lead between the silent houses, and at the top of the village stands the sixteenth-century church of the Pantokrator with an integral belfry and a tiny apse; it contains some of the best-preserved frescoes on Corfu and the main part of the church is usually locked, but it may be possible to have it opened by asking in the village. Lower down is Agios Merkourios: this eleventh-century Byzantine church is the most historic on the island after that of SS Jason and Sosipater in Anemomylos and also contains some very ancient paintings.

A few metres from the Agios Markos turning a second road to the left leads up to Spartilas, Strinilas and the summit of Mt Pantokrator (this is the road used for the return journey at the end of this route). The coastal road now descends briefly through olive groves towards the newish resort of Barbati, before climbing again, so that Nissaki, the next community, is several hundred metres below. **Barbati** has a long, narrow beach composed of large white pebbles with smaller golden shingle at the water's edge; there are a couple of hotels, several villas, and a watersports centre; boats ply regularly between it and Ipsos. Beyond Barbati lie a string of beaches at the foot of the mountain, attractively situated but, as the road continues to ascend, increasingly arduous of access. **Glyfa**, 2 km beyond Barbati, has another pebble strand reached by a steep path from the main road; 2 km further on, **Nissaki** presents several ways down to its beach, all of them extremely steep – the taverna 'Vitamins' on the main road here may strike visitors as offering just what they need after the long haul back up from the sea! Nissaki, in fact, offers access to several beaches, all of pebble, shingle or rocks but scenic and well worth the effort involved in reaching them: there are *tavernas* and a few shops, as well as watersport and boat-hiring facilities – this is a good place from which to explore the many small coves and beaches to the north. There is also a regular boat service to and from Corfu Town in summer. The Club Mediterranée occupies its own beach here too, while a pebbly cove with fine shingle at the water's edge north of the village is dominated by the large Nissaki Beach Hotel. Between the two, down a concrete track, lies the pleasant little cove of **Kaminaki**, where a huddle of attractive villas have a small beach of fine shingle to themselves. From Kaminaki it is possible to walk along the coast to Kouloura along easy paths – and right round the island's north-eastern corner to

Kassiopi if you have the time (about 4 hours) and energy. Another spectacular walk from Nissaki (a far more arduous one) is the hike up the mountain to the deserted village of Sinies, begun up a minor road signposted Viglatsouri by the Nissaki bus shelter. From here one can go on to climb to the summit of Pantokrator (a taxing ascent – it is wise to tell someone of your intentions in advance in case of accidents). This route is fully described in *The Corfu Book of Walks*, widely available on the island.

Leaving Nissaki, there is a petrol station to the left (before the Kaminaki access track) as the road continues through the villages of Kendroma and Guimari, recognisable by its pretty belfry, festooned with fairy lights, standing beside the road. Again, both have small beaches of pebbles to which steep paths offer access, but since the road is now about 600m above sea level there are few takers: most of the customers of the *tavernas* on steeply shelving Agni beach below have arrived by boat or walked along the coast (these unfrequented beaches provide a popular barbecue stop for boat excursions also).

Some 12 km along the coastal corniche from Pyrgi, we are well into the area the guides like to call 'Durrell Country'; here a turning to the right leads down to the sea once more, this time to the villages of Kouloura and Kalami, one on each side of the Karagol Point. There are spectacular views of both from the main road above, and of the Albanian coast, the mountains and Lake Butrinto being clearly visible on all but the haziest days.

To visit Kalami and Kouloura take the turning off the main coastal road described above; at a fork in the road, a left turn brings you into the small fishing village of **Kouloura**, lying in peaceful isolation at the foot of a hillside that is covered with yellow broom in spring and early summer. There is a small amount of parking under the trees by the road. The village centres on a picturesque harbour and comprises a *taverna*, a row of cottages and a fortified Venetian villa with a chapel. In season there may be boats for hire. The beach, minute and pebbly, lies down a rough track to the north of the harbour under large eucalyptus and ilex trees. Returning to the fork and going straight on will bring you after less than 1 km to **Kalami**, where the road ends (limited parking). More developed than Kouloura, Kalami was a remote fishing village within living memory but is nowadays a popular place for villa holidays; there are shops, as well as half a dozen restaurants and bars. Here the White House 'set like a dice on a rock already venerable with the scars of wind and water' where Lawrence Durrell lived and wrote *Prospero's Cell* in 1939 still stands, prominent at the water's edge at the far end of the bay:

Lawrence Durrell's White House at Kalami

nowadays it houses a pleasant *taverna* with a vine-shaded terrace, while the accommodation above has been divided into two holiday flats. Despite the new building, the bay remains beautiful. Cypress-clad headlands enclose it and the barren coastline of Albania appears very close across the strait. The beach, which generally becomes crowded only in the height of summer, shelves gently, with pebbly shingle, a little sand at the water's edge and occasional flat rocks; the usual range of watersports is available in season.

A viewpoint a few metres beyond the Kalami/Kouloura turning offers an opportunity to park and enjoy the fabulous views of Albania only 2½ km away, and to look down onto the unspoilt stretch of Corfiot coastline below: a large tract of the land below you is owned by the Rothschild family. Wonderful views continue, as the road remains at a high level, passing the village of Agnitsini (where a track leads down to yet another shingle beach) and, about 4 km from the Kalami/Kouloura turning, another opportunity to go down to the coast, this time to the up-and-coming resort of Agios Stefanos (San Stefano).

From this turning a pleasantly verdant, shady (and at the time of writing almost completely metalled) road makes its way onto the remote headland at Corfu's north-eastern corner. There are fine views of the deep cove of **Agios Stefanos** as you approach. The resort itself projects an air of casual opulence; magnificent roses bloom in the gardens and besides a growing number of villas, there are at least six restaurants and a cocktail bar. The beach itself, punctuated by half a dozen landing stages, is safe for children, but narrow and gravelly; the setting is tranquil and beautiful, however. Caiques call regularly en route to Corfu town, and the bay is visited by several boat excursions from elsewhere, as well as by private yachts in high season. From Agios Stefanos a track leads southwards to the less developed white pebble beach of Kerasia, where there are a few villas and a single taverna. Also reachable from Agios Stefanos are a number of little-visited pebble beaches to the north: this north-eastern headland, Cape Varvara, has only ceased to be a military reserve relatively recently and little development has taken place here as yet; a scattering of villas have beaches such as Avlaki and the large sweep (excellent for windsurfing, with a stiff midday onshore breeze) at Koyevinas almost to themselves.

The main road now winds through thickly wooded countryside in which the Judas trees are spectacular in spring and the ubiquitous dark cypresses form dramatic vertical accents. Some 4 km after the Agios Stefanos turning (there is a petrol station on this stretch) the ancient and substantial village of **Kassiopi** is reached, entered by a slip road off to the right which terminates in a surprisingly large north-facing harbour area.

Kassiopi enjoys an attractive setting, and although it is these days a popular resort which can be noisy and unpleasantly crowded in high summer it has not yet been quite overwhelmed by commercialism, remaining more 'Greek' than many of Corfu's tourist centres. Founded in 360 BC as a colony of Corinth, it became a substantial settlement in Roman times – when Cicero, Cato, Mark Antony and the Emperor Nero were among its distinguished visitors.

On the hill to the west of the harbour stand the ruins of a castle built by the Angevins in the thirteenth century, itself a remodelling of earlier fortifications begun by the Romans, then enlarged by the Normans – when the Venetians acquired control of Corfu one of their first acts was to dismantle this castle for fear that their rivals the Genoese would seize it. Kassiopi also possesses an unusually attractive church, built on the site of an ancient temple of Jupiter (where Nero is said to have given a song recital) which later became an early Christian basilica. Just behind the harbour (on the western side) the Church of Panagia Kassiopitissa (Our Lady of Kassiopi) was for long esteemed by Corfiots as the most important shrine on the island (until the cult of St Spiridon supplanted it): it has been associated with a number of miracles (notably the healing of a youth who had been unjustly blinded as a punishment for stealing some flour in 1530) and the silver-cased icon of the Virgin to the right of the altar used at one time to be regularly saluted by passing ships. Today the tiny building is a blaze of colour and light. Approached from the main street via a belfried gate, under a bower of wistaria and through a minute, crowded graveyard, the ornamental interior glows like a

Kassiopi harbour

jewel; fragments of 17th-century frescoes are exposed in the lower walls of the sanctuary.

Kassiopi's harbour with its cannons, mobile post office and several bars is a lively centre. There are boat hire facilities and a number of excursions as well as a daily boat service to Corfu Town; there is also generous parking space. But there is plenty of evidence that the harbour is still used by working fishermen as well. Albania (from which not a few refugees have settled in Kassiopi) dominates the horizon in almost every direction, the lighthouse on Kapareli Island prominent in mid-channel.

From the eastern end of the harbour it is possible to walk along the coast from the Eucalyptus bar. At the other end a path signposted 'to the beach' gives glimpses of Avlaki, an extensive white pebbly beach to the east, as it wanders past Indian bead trees, eucalyptus and cypresses; there is bathing from rocky shelves as the path passes below some imposing villas before ascending to the overgrown main gateway and walls of the ruined castle. This path culminates at the Restaurant/bar Kastro Kassiopi where there is a small promontory with an east-facing beach of steeply shelving white pebbles; another sickle-shaped north-facing beach lies a little further on (pedaloes, sunbeds and watersports available in high season). The main town beach, shelving steeply and once again of somewhat uncomfortable pebbles, lies to the west of the village beside the main road.

After Kassiopi the landscape changes. The northern foothills of Mt Pantokrator are softer and less craggy and there are no more olive groves, just rocky hills with a thin covering of grass and scrub, studded with thousands of asphodel and lit up in May and June by golden splashes of broom: several now deserted hamlets can be found by wanderers on these bleak slopes. The road clings to the coast along the Bay of Apraos (or Imerolia), passing two small pebbly beaches and a large shallow stretch of pale sand –

Kalamaki, the first truly sandy beach north of Corfu Town – in front of an area of wetland at the northern end. About 6 km from Kassiopi a turning to the left ascends the northern slopes of Mt Pantokrator, leading eventually to the haunting mountain village of **Old Perithia**, now almost entirely deserted, in a hollow below the peak.

To visit the village, take this left turn which enters the village of Nea Perithia almost immediately. (There are ancient caves nearby where Stone Age settlements have been discovered.) Here fork left, following signs for Loutses and Ano Perithia, and keep bearing left and uphill as the road climbs towards the pretty, sprawling village of Loutses, alive with birdsong. Thereafter the countryside rapidly becomes rockier and wilder, with a scattering of wild pears and smooth green hills ahead. About 1 km out of Loutses the road deteriorates to the extent that only sturdy vehicles can continue with any comfort; the walk from here, however, is enjoyable and only takes about 35 minutes. The track goes up the side of a long valley heading straight into the heart of the Pantokrator massif, the peak itself appearing soon after the path leaves the valley and levels out. After about half an hour's walking the first houses of Old Perithia come into view in a fold to your right and the path continues towards them past orchards of almond, pear and cherry.

Although many of the houses are now falling into decay, Perithia offers a fascinating and authentic insight into the nature of an eighteenth-century Corfiot village, right down to the absence of wheeled traffic. The buildings are well-constructed of stone in the Venetian style. In addition to no less than seven churches the remains of walls surrounding the village are visible, and a watchtower from which the inhabitants could keep an eye out against any possibility of pirates or other seaborne invaders. The silence is broken only by birdsong and

Ruined houses at Old Perithia, Mt Pantokrator
in the background

the sporadic tinkling of sheep bells from the several flocks that roam the remote hillsides around. A stroll around the grassy 'streets' is an eerie and atmospheric experience: sheep huddle in the shade of a church belfry and it is possible to view the interiors of some of the old houses – but take care, many have rotten floorboards, and one building which was clearly the school seems on the verge of final collapse. Perithia is not quite deserted, however: a few inhabitants remain, and during the summer months a café is usually open.

The walk back down to your car offers superb views of the Albanian coast and (unless the day is hazy) of the offshore Corfiot islets of Erikoussa and the somewhat larger Othoni. The whole walk to Perithia and back can be done in little over an hour, but those interested in butterflies, flowers and birds are liable to find themselves distracted over and over again by new varieties spotted from the path.

Returning to the main coastal road, some 200 m further on another diversion may be made, this time to the pretty little beach of Agios Spiridon and the lagoon of Andinioti.

Here a turning to the right (signposted 'Beach of Saint Spyridion') winds through shady olive groves past a few villas to a delightful beach by a small chapel. Usually quiet (except in high season and at weekends when it is often thronged with Corfiots), **Agios Spiridon** beach is sandy and shelves gently into a shallow sea – ideal for young children. The setting is tranquil and beautiful: butterflies abound and behind the main beach, beside a large Judas tree, the tiny chapel is alive with birds which nest in the corrugations of the roof. To the east a track leads over a grassy promontory to another small sandy beach and a rocky cove where people fish, overlooking a small tree-capped islet.

At the western end of the beach, where sea holly and sea daffodils grow in profusion, a channel flows out to the sea from the Andinioti lagoon. Known as Antiniotissa ('Death of Youth' – perhaps a reference to the mosquitoes that then flourished here) until recent times, the lagoon is a popular venue for duck-shooting in the autumn and the surrounding reed beds teem with bird life. This is the place where the young Gerald Durrell spent happy hours specimen-hunting while his older brother banged away at the waterfowl at the other end of the lagoon. A bridge across the channel leads on over Cape Agios Ekaterinis, an area ablaze with wild flowers in spring. The view inland is impressive, though somewhat marred by a large white factory building: the northern slopes of Mt Pantokrator rise, fold on fold, and on the peak the radio masts are clearly visible.

There is as yet a single *taverna* at Agios Spiridon, but it seems inevitable that tourist development will reach here soon. After a swim at Agios Spiridon a right turn in the olive groves takes you past a cemetery to rejoin the coastal road a few hundred metres west of the point where you left it.

Westwards from here the coastal road is broad, fast and level, running as it does along a flat coastal plain between the Pantokrator foothills and the dunes backing the 7-km long sweep of beach that runs along Corfu's northern seaboard from Cape Agios Ekaterinis to Roda and beyond. This sandy strip is accessible at several points along the road, notably at 'Almiros Beach' some 2 km after leaving Agios Spiridon, where there is a *taverna* and a small amount of development.

Our route, however, leaves the coast 2 km further on at Acharavi, a small town whose inhabitants clearly feel deprived of their fair share of Corfu's tourist trade – a large notice informs the visitor that 'all the shops of our area are equally as good as in other areas'. At the roundabout as you enter the town, make a left turn onto Eleutherias St and pursue a minor road through the outskirts, turning right at the edge of the village. (An alternative route by a faster road, but missing the opportunity to visit Mt Pantokrator's summit, can be used by turning left 200 m further on through Agios Pandeleimon and Episkepsis, an attractive village with a fine Venetian manor house; shortly after Sgourades a left turn leads up to Strinilas and Mt Pantokrator, while carrying straight on brings you to Spartilas and Pyrgi as described on p.138.) From here a newly surfaced road climbs gently towards the village of Agios Martinos, where it bears right, becoming steeper with magnificent views of the Pantokrator foothills and, from some of the bends, the offshore islands. About 5 km from Acharavi it enters Lavki, a remote hill village with two churches and a tiny square. In this beautiful and little visited area the vegetation has not changed for centuries. Before the Venetians encouraged olive cultivation so forcefully the whole island probably looked like this: some fine oaks still border the road, and though forest fires have claimed many of their number, the blaze of Spanish broom in early summer more than compensates for the slightly bumpy ride.

About half an hour up from the coast, the lonely village of Petalia is reached, a patch of grey-brown and terracotta huddled into the mountainside. The surrounding slopes have been laboriously terraced, some for vineyards. Just beyond the village a turning to the left (signed '**Pantokrator**') offers the opportunity to visit the top of the mountain whose bulk has dominated the landscape throughout the route.

The way to the summit commences as a well-metalled road, and one day soon, no doubt, it will be possible for any vehicle to drive all the way in comfort. At the time of writing, however, the surface soon degenerates, becoming a rough track; this is drivable with care, but on the final stretch (after 3 km or so) its surface is extremely rough and unstable, and drivers of all but the most sturdy vehicles would be well advised to undertake the assault on the steep, slippery hairpins of the final mound on foot (about 25 mins). The rocky landscape by the road offers much to interest the botanist – wild flowers and rock plants abound in spring and early summer, including fritillaries, dwarf irises and orchids. The monastery itself, dedicated to the 'Pantokrator' (the Almighty), is largely a nineteenth-century remodelling of a seventeenth-century building and stands on the site of the original mountain-top church, erected in 1347 (and paid for by the villagers of 27 surrounding settlements): there may have been a temple of Zeus up here in ancient times (when the mountain was known as Mount Istone), though no trace of one has been found. Today the building is unoccupied except during the festival of the Transfiguration (6 August), one of the most important on the island. Until recent times this feast day (*panagia*) was observed by Corfiots from all over the northern part of the island who would walk to the summit during the night and use the cells which ring the monastery courtyard. The building suffers from the proximity of the enormous red and white communications aerial which dominates the conical summit, but there is a welcome well of cool water for visitors to avail themselves of, and the views from the summit are, as one would expect, spectacular: on a good day the panorama includes Paxos and Cefalonia to the south, as well as most of Corfu itself, Albania and Lake Butrinto to the east, Old Perithia and the offshore islands of Othoni and Erikoussa to the north, and to the north-west Mathraki: it is claimed that on *very* clear days you can even see the heel of Italy.

Back at the junction outside Petalia the metalled surface returns almost immediately (this is the road used by the tourist coaches) and Strinilas is soon entered, its houses perched picturesquely on rocks, with an attractive bar and café in the shade of a large elm tree; the village is surrounded by neatly terraced fields and, lower down, the vineyards which are the source of the medium-sweet local wine, thought by some to be Corfu's best. Passing a communications station on your right, you will see immediately afterwards why it is there: for a bend to the left suddenly reveals a breath-taking panorama of the whole of the southern part of the island. From here the road descends gently towards a T-junction at which you should turn left for Spartilas, which is entered shortly after; this ancient village's narrow main street, lined with small houses painted in pastel colours and with an appealing baroque church, winds along a natural balcony with more marvellous, almost aerial, views down to the sea and beyond. From here the road descends in a series of tight hairpin bends to reach the coastal road just outside Pyrgi 5 km later. From here follow the road back to Corfu Town.

TOURING CORFU

2: *The North-West*

This corner of Corfu offers a pleasant variety of landscapes, though few are as dramatic as those around Mount Pantokrator. Its attractions include superb views from the Troumpeta pass, the impressive fortress of Angelokastro, some burgeoning beach resorts (Sidari and Roda on the flat north coast, Arilas and Agios Stefanos on the west), pretty hill villages and, in the superbly situated Ag. Georgiou Bay, a strong contender for the title of Corfu's loveliest beach.

Many visitors to Corfu make a special excursion to Paleokastritsa; in this book it is described as part of Route 3 (pp.150–1), but a visit to Paleokastritsa could easily be combined with this route if desired.

Leave Corfu Town on the Paleokastritsa road as for route 1 and continue past Kontokali and Gouvia to the junction at Tsavros, where the road for Dasia and the north-east coast goes off to the right. Here keep straight on, following the broad, attractive road originally built by British soldiers – the story is that the second British Lord High Commissioner, Sir Frederick Adam, was inordinately fond of Paleokastritsa but found the journey tedious, so he contrived to get the British army to construct the road by the ingenious expedient of first establishing a military convalescent home there.

About 4 km from the Tsavros junction ignore a turning to Sidari and Roda to the right and keep straight on: 2 km further down the road is the Mavromatis distillery, where a wide variety of local liqueurs can be tasted (and purchased, of course), many of them variants of *koumkouat*. The first signs of Paleokastritsa are reached some 12 km from the Tsavros junction. If you are visiting the resort at this stage follow the road into town, otherwise take the right fork to Lakones near the Disco Paleo in the outskirts.

This road climbs steeply through terraced olive groves – on one of the bends an elderly gentleman is often stationed, offering bags of delicious, if pricey, almonds. Glorious views shortly appear to the left, and after some 3 km **Lakones** is reached, an ancient settlement strung out along a ridge high above the coves and promontories of Paleokastritsa, which was 'colonized' from here. Lakones, once famous for its dry red wine, is about halfway up Mt Arakli, at 405 m Corfu's third highest mountain; a magnificent, if fairly strenuous, walk to the summit begins at a flight of steps near the entrance to the village opposite a cafe whose balcony offers 'A Nice View' – bear right at the top of the steps and allow 2½–3 hours.

For the best views, proceed through Lakones (past the small Alikes workshop specializing in olive wood carvings) to the popular Bella Vista café 2 km further on. Here you can have a cool drink or a snack under a Judas tree and feel on top of the world, with unbeatable views of the monastery, Paleokastritsa's bays and coves and the headlands to the south, Cape Agios Iliodoros and Plaka point (with several remote and inaccessible beaches in between).

A kilometre beyond the Bella Vista, just before the village of Makrades begins, take a minor road to the left to visit the hill fortress of **Angelokastro**, whose craggy bulk you may already have glimpsed on the road from Lakones. The climb to the summit is much less arduous than it looks and takes only some 20 minutes each way. A short way down this road is the quiet and unspoilt little village of Krini, boasting two belfries, one white painted and one stone: keep straight on at the central 'roundabout' (a tree!) and park on waste ground opposite the café/bar Panorama or where you can; then follow the track out of the village, bearing right at the first fork. A few minutes later the castle appears, impregnably perched 400 metres up on its rocky crag. Built on the orders of Michael Angelos Comnenos, Despot of Epirus, in the thirteenth century, Angelokastro and the Old Fort in Corfu Town were the only strongholds that Barbarossa's Turkish army was unable to subdue in 1537 – on which occasion at least 3000 Corfiots saved their lives and their liberty by taking refuge within its massive walls; indeed the citadel, which is so sited as to be able to see (and send signals to) Corfu Town, has never been taken in all its long and turbulent history.

When the track forks, do not be tempted by a narrow path heading straight towards the castle (it is rough and very prickly); instead bear left down a broad track lined with white and pink cistus, spartium and Jerusalem sage. After five minutes the path begins to climb, past a vertiginous cliff towards a fork: to the left a perilous path skirts the outside of the eminence, with stunning views of Mount Arakli, Paleokastritsa and the sea below, until it reaches a point where only the most foolhardy or nerveless would risk continuing. To the right another path leads to the entrance to the outer keep. Inside, pink convulvulus and enormous yellow mullein flourishes, but little remains of the fortress, apart from an almost intact cistern: on the summit the small wooden-ceilinged chapel of the Archangels Michael and Gabriel (last rebuilt in 1784) is still in periodic use and nearby, curious hollows in the rock suggest shallow tombs – at least one is shaped like a man in armour. Elsewhere there are hints of underground chambers and lower down, near the inner courtyard, is the cave chapel of Ag. Kyriaki: inside are hermit cells carved from the rock and vestigial frescoes.

Return through Krini to the main road, reached just outside the rather larger village of Makrades (to your left), a huddle of tiled roofs, many covering buildings in the Venetian style with arched doorways and stuccoed frontages in pastel shades: a steep track from Makrades (unsuitable for motor vehicles for most of its length) leads down to Ag. Georgiou Bay. For the passing motorist Makrades offers a rather alarming local speciality: importunate stallholders by the road who will make every effort to get you to look at the herbs and honey they have for sale, sometimes even leaping out into the middle of the road and waving maps to detain you!

Having escaped the predatory Makradians, continue to the next village, Vistonas. (If you cannot wait to reach the beach, a rough track down to Ag. Georgiou via the pretty village of Prinilas goes off to the left just before Vistonas, but there are much better roads further on.) The road surface is patchy at this point, but the hillsides are so thick with heather in autumn and Spanish broom in spring, it is like driving along an ornamental avenue. Olive groves are conspicuous by their absence: instead, vineyards and small market gardens surround the villages as the road climbs, hugging the northern contours of Mount Arakli with fine views to the north and west. In the far distance Corfu's three inhabited offshore islands, Othoni, Mathraki and Erikoussa, are visible: there are occasional intriguing glimpses of the east coast, too, and numerous villages come into view, often set on high ground among the rolling hills, a reminder that Corfu's 209 villages make it one of the most densely populated of the Greek islands. As recently as 1969, much of this corner of the island was inaccessible to motorists.

Passing the turning to Alimatades on the left, the road now snakes down to the Troumpeta pass, reached about 9 km from Makrades. At the pass, where Corfu Town becomes distantly visible to the south-east, turn left and continue to descend on the main Sidari road (ignoring a turning to Roda) for some 3 km, until a large sign on the left announces a turning to Ag. Georgiou beach. This is the best of the routes to the southern end of this magnificent bay and

Peaceful Pagi

a diversion here (of about 15 km) is well worth making, particularly if it is time for a swim.

This turning (also signposted for Pagi and Prinilas) takes you straight into the village of Arkadades, after which a good metalled road winds downhill, crossing and recrossing a small river as it follows the contours, first through olive groves then through slopes of bracken and wild flowers. Passing the small village of Vatonies, half-hidden among cypress and fruit trees, the road proceeds under lofty limestone crags as it approaches Pagi, where the remains of a Roman villa were found in the last century. Set among almond trees, Pagi is a timeless settlement: its traditional belfry is festooned with coloured lights, the scent of freshly baked bread fills the air and massive redundant millstones lie around the village. At the far end bear right to reach the sea (straight on would take you to Prinilas).

Earlier guidebooks invariably bemoaned the inevitability of **Ag. Georgiou bay** succumbing to touristic development, and within the last few years the process has got well under way, with new buildings going up all the time. Nevertheless the bay's magnificent setting can never be entirely ruined: it is enclosed by two glorious headlands, Cape Arilla to the north and Cape Falakron, its lower slopes covered with olive and cypress (and ablaze with Spanish broom in spring), to the south. The beach itself is one of Corfu's finest, some 3 km long and still relatively unspoilt: a golden stretch of slightly coarse sand with some shingle and a belt of larger pebbles at the edge, where the water gets deep quite quickly. Behind it are a number of bars and tavernas, a scattering of villas and hotels and a small church. As well as umbrellas, sunbeds and pedaloes, there are facilities for motorboat hire, jet-skiing and windsurfing. A sandy track runs along the back of the beach, but fails to reach the far end, access to which is gained either on foot or from the road to Afionas (see p.145); a small stream forms a pool full of frogs (which can be highly vocal in the evenings!) and terrapins before running under the beach. Return to the main road the way you came, turning left after Arkadades to resume the route.

At Agros, 1 km further on, leave the Sidari road and fork left (signposted Dafni and Kavadades) through Manatades and Aspiotades (which boasts an unusual square-topped castellated belfry). The road follows the contours of the hills, winding through olive groves with occasional glimpses of Ag. Georgiou bay and Cape Arilla to the left. Dafni, reached about 4 km from the Agros turn-off, is another widely spaced settlement, lying along a ridge with panoramic views. Lemon, orange and apricot trees grow around it, as well as vines and the ubiquitous olives (there is a petrol station just past the village). Leaving Dafni there is a track down to Ag. Georgiou beach, but the better road continues to Armenades, a sizeable village of slightly shabby houses on a thickly wooded slope, then bears left to Kavadades on top of the opposite slope where there is a T-junction. (The typical -ades ending to place names in Corfu simply means 'place' and corresponds to the -ata ending common elsewhere in Greece.) Here go left (signposted Afiona) and climb steeply out of the village onto a ridge. (Rough tracks off to the left here lead to the beach, but are best ignored unless you have four-wheel drive.) Follow the metalled road towards Afionas, where for those who wish to return to the beach there is a short and partially metalled road (signposted to the Golden Moon Restaurant) which leads down to the northern end of the bay just before a four-storeyed apartment building in the village.

Afionas itself is well worth a visit, and the walk onto Cape Arilla that can be done from here is a must. The village sprawls along its headland, with a small square containing the church at the far end. To do the walk (which takes less than an hour) park here if you can and take a path (not steps) that leaves the square from the corner opposite to the road; keep bearing left as the track becomes a rocky path along the left hand edge of the headland – the tiny fields to your left offer tempting picnic spots with wonderful views of the bay below. Soon the path emerges from the trees; pick your way, continuing to bear left and downwards between clumps of heather and small pink cistus bushes whose scent fills the air on windless days. At one point the path becomes confused but it can easily be found again if you keep aiming forward and down. On the narrow isthmus at the bottom of the path twin small beaches of fine shingle with very shallow water provide a choice of bathing spots depending on wind direction. Small boats are moored in the shelter of the little cove opposite: this tiny harbour used to be known as Port Timone (meaning 'a tiller'). The promontory beyond is covered in dense maquis, but you can wander a little further on to it if you wish, up a rudimentary path leading towards the ruined house on the northern side. Remains of Neolithic settlements, perhaps 8000 years old, have been found on this peninsula, and some commentators on the *Odyssey* have suggested Afionas with its twin harbours as the site of Alcinous' palace (see also pp.64–5) – perhaps Nausicaa washed the clothes in the stream flowing into Ag. Georgiou bay and maybe Gravia island to the north should be identified with Odysseus' petrified ship (*karavi* means a ship in Greek).

Back at Afionas, one can explore the old part of the village by walking up the steps opposite the church; from the top there are good views of Gravia and the Bay of Arilla to the north with the offshore islands and Albania in the distance. Leaving the village turn left after 1 km for Arilas. The landscape here is gently pastoral, with lush rather northern vegetation – bracken, brambles and meadow grasses. A few new-looking villas are dotted about, their frequency increasing as the road descends towards **Arilas**, 6 km further on. This is a remote and pleasantly low-key resort behind a long but narrow beach of fine golden sand and shingle, gently shelving and ideal for families with young children. The village has a few restaurants, bars and shops, a disco and a couple of hotels, one of which, the Arilla Inn, claims to have been founded in 1867. The road behind the beach leads nowhere, so return through the village from the jetty which bisects the beach and turn left at the first opportunity, then left again at the top of the hill by the Arillas Star cafeteria and a shrine (there is a petrol station 200m further on). This road soon becomes metalled again and takes you out across the next headland to **Agios Stefanos** (or, as it is still often called, San Stefano).

This resort, flanked by the small cape of the same name, is another once-quiet spot that is rapidly becoming developed; the untidy sprawl of new buildings suggest it is directing its appeal to the young and, predominantly, the British. The beach is a long broad arc of sand and pebbles, with rocks out to sea and a tendency for seaweed to build up in the centre. It is popular with windsurfers. A church with a stunted belfry stands at the far end of the village: beyond it a track leads to the tip of the headland, which is in fact Corfu's (and Greece's, if we exclude the offshore islets) most westerly point.

Leaving Agios Stefanos and continuing northwards (now signposted Kerkyra), the road climbs through pretty countryside in which a rash of villas have appeared in recent years. Out to sea two islands are visible: the smaller and nearer is Diaplo with the much larger Mathraki looming behind. At the peaceful hill village of Avliotes, the road turns inland descending an avenue of Judas trees towards a small intensively cultivated valley. About 3 km beyond Avliotes, another worthwhile diversion (4 km) to the coast is possible where a left turn is signposted to **Peroulades.**

Taking this turning leads you to the unusual Peroulades beaches and also provides an opportunity to explore the attractive scenery of Cape Drastis on foot. To reach the beaches keep right at a fork at the end of this rather dilapidated village and follow signs (variously spelt) to the Sunset Taverna, turning right again at an old disused pump. An open area under a cliff of sandy marl soon appears, in which one can park and proceed down a concrete path which leads to a flight of steps. On either side of these stretches a perfect, if narrow, beach of fine dark gold sand with shallow water, spectacularly backed by towering sheer cliffs of striated clay/packed earth varying in colour from golden to grey – a marked contrast to Corfu's more usual limestone. For all their apparent remoteness these beaches are surprisingly popular, even crowded at weekends – they are within easy cycling distance of Sidari.

Back in Peroulades a track from the church leads to Cape Drastis: it passes the school building and soon descends towards the sea, past a precipitous viewpoint to an attractive cove (allow about 1 hour for the walk). Cape Drastis is Corfu's north-western tip: the cape, the eroded rocks offshore and a small arch standing in the sea produce a natural spectacle slightly reminiscent of the Dorset coast.

Back on the main road, it is only 2 km to **Sidari**, an increasingly popular but still unsophisticated resort; there are no large hotels as yet, but the village is growing fast along its single street. The large beach lies on the left as you approach Sidari: composed of fine firm powdery dark sand (ideal for buckets and spades), it is very deep but slightly scruffy with fragments of weed and offers little shade apart from an area at the western end (where there is a small planting of eucalyptus). There is a full range of facilities, with patrolling ice cream vendors, sunbeds and umbrellas available at various points along the beach, pedaloes and canoes for hire and watersports (including parascending). It is possible to canoe from here to Cape Drastis or round to Peroulades, and there are several boat excursions available, including trips to Erikoussa and the other offshore islands. The water is extremely shallow and often so warm as to be unrefreshing; ideal for small children, it is frustrating for more energetic swimmers. These are better advised to head further west, to the headland beyond the bay, which is accessible either on foot from the back of the main beach or by a small track from the road. Here Sidari's main claims to fame are to be found, a series of strange rock formations, interestingly striated and eroded; the rock here is a mixture of soft sandstone and marl, and has been moulded by erosion into ledges and caves which offer more entertaining and adventurous conditions for serious swimmers than the main beach. There are perfect small beaches to explore in this region, with sandstone stacks and tiny islets to give interest to the view. The most famous rock formation here is the celebrated '*Canal d'Amour*', a channel (once a tunnel, until the roof caved in) of which legend has it that a maiden who swims its full length when it is in shade will win the man of her dreams.

From Sidari the main road turns due south, back towards Corfu Town via the Troumpeta pass. The north-western tour can be continued, however, by taking a longer route along the north coast and turning inland at Roda, whence the road south skirts the lowest foothills of Mount Pantokrator. Unless you are in a hurry to get home, therefore, ignore the signs to Kerkyra in the middle of Sidari and drive straight on along the back of the beach and through the main tourist strip, busy with bicycles and pedestrians. From here follow signs to Karoussades and Roda, along a road that goes a little way inland at first but soon bends left to follow the coastline. This largely flat area of Corfu has been inhabited for millennia, as the discovery of Neolithic pottery and tools here proves: it has always been fertile and well-watered and agriculture is still the mainstay of local life. The plain meets the sea in a thin strip of sand and shingle, which is really an extension of Sidari beach. Along the shore are a series of minimally developed beaches reachable from the road by rough tracks over the dunes: Agios Ioannis is one such, and Astrakeri, facing east and north on the cape of the same name, has a larger stretch of sand and shingle backed by grey cliffs, as well as several restaurants reached by roads and tracks to the left of the main road. The area is clearly a contender for further development – at present its attractions are few, apart from the opportunities for solitude offered by its beaches.

Inland from Astrakeri is the unassuming village of **Karoussades**, the largest in this corner of the island, set in a small range of hills: with a number of old and elegant stuccoed houses, and no tourist trappings, the village is a reminder of the 'real' Corfu on which resorts such as Sidari and Roda have little impact. Its main showpiece is the fortified mansion of the celebrated Theotokis family (see p.119), who made their country home here – parts of it are fifteenth-century. The sixteenth-century church of Agia Katherini is also of interest, with some surviving wall paintings, and at Kavalouri, a little further south, there is another fine old Venetian country house.

Four km to the west lies the resort of **Roda**, once a tiny fishing hamlet at the western end of the longest beach on the island: it stretches for almost 6 km. The outline of a Doric temple of the fifth century BC has been excavated here – fragments of it can be seen in the archaeological museum in Corfu Town – and there may be further antiquities to be found. The large Roda Beach Hotel at the extreme western tip is old-established, but the rest of the resort is almost entirely new and still being developed – with, it must be said, unimpressive results. The beach itself, reached by taking a left turn at the central roundabout which leads to a promenade, is a long slim rather wild stretch of powdery sand, with a belt of pebbles at the edge and some weed; as at Sidari, the water is shallow for quite a long way out, but the enormous length of the beach makes it hard to imagine that it could ever become unpleasantly overcrowded, it being always possible to walk further east to guarantee seclusion. Less smart and less popular than Sidari, Roda nevertheless offers a full range of tourist facilities – including car/bike rental, minimarkets, hotels, *tavernas*, etc. The setting is flat and unspectacular, though the beginnings of the Pantokrator range are visible, looming to the east.

From Roda, three alternative routes back to the capital present themselves: continuing along the same road will bring you at length to Kassiopi and round the north-eastern part of the island, as described in the first part of Route 1; or it is possible to follow this road a little way then turn right at Acharavi, returning to Corfu via Episkepsis and Spartilas, as in the second stage of that route. For the purposes of completing a north-western circuit, however, turn inland at Roda, following signs to Kerkyra from the roundabout.

The road south passes through a series of attractive and unspoilt villages: Sfakera, the first, is a pretty little community containing a fortified Venetian mansion near the central square which still retains its gun-mountings and iron grilles. At Platonas, 2 km further on, there is a last opportunity for a diversion (signposted) to see the abandoned monastery at Nimfes.

> This dignified village is set among trees and gardens some 3 km off the main road. **Nimfes** is celebrated for its gushing fountain and also for the abandoned monastery of Pantokrator standing in a tranquil grove of cypresses close by the cave of the hermit Artemios on the northern outskirts of the village. There are fine walks in this area. To rejoin the main Roda-Troumpeta road, simply continue through the village for a further 2 km to Episkopi.

The hill villages of Xathates, Episkopi, Agii Douli (which also has some exceptionally attractive Venetian houses) and Choroepiskopi are soon passed as the countryside gradually becomes more mountainous and craggy. A quarry unpleasantly scars the landscape (you may have seen it from as far away as Afionas) and the road climbs steeply; 19 km from Roda, the road meets the one from Sidari coming in from the right (at a potentially hazardous junction) for the final ascent to the Troumpeta pass. Bearing left at the top, superb views of the east coast and Corfu Town soon appear, and for a brief period both sides of the island are visible at once as the road descends in broad lazy sweeps.

The village of Skripero, 3 km down the slope, is worth a look as you pass by – it contains some of the finest arcaded village houses on the island. Further on a turning to the left leads through the large village of Ano Korakiana, from which the resorts of the north-east coast can quickly be reached without the necessity of returning to Corfu Town; if you are based south of the capital you may prefer to turn off the road for Doukades just *before* reaching Skripero, and make your way back via the Ropa Plain, Pelekas and the west coast. The main road back to Corfu Town (14 km) joins the Paleokastritsa road 4 km south of Skripero, from which the journey back is simply a matter of bearing right at the Sgombou and Tsavros junctions.

TOURING CORFU

3: *Paleokastritsa and the West*

This tour commences in exactly the same way as Route 2, following the east coast as far as Tsavros, where it runs inland to traverse the island on the fine scenic route to Paleokastritsa first marked out by Sir Frederick Adam's engineers in the 1820s. Instead of turning uphill to Lakones when the coast is reached, however, drive on into Paleokastritsa itself.

Paleokastritsa's fame as a beauty spot is widespread, and its beaches and idyllic setting have made it one of Corfu's most popular resorts. A cluster of picturesque coves backed by tree-clad hills and the soaring cliff on which stands the fortress of Angelokastro, Paleokastritsa was never a village, merely the port of Lakones, sited further up the hill where it was less likely to fall a prey to pirates.

Today the celebrated landscape is overlaid with buildings clinging to the hillside, the once lonely coves are crowded with bathers and visitors and the road swarms with a constant stream of traffic bearing day-trippers. Anyone who knew Paleokastritsa a generation ago will undoubtedly find the recent overdevelopment of this once perfect spot profoundly depressing, but for first-timers 'the conspiracy of light, air, blue sea and cypresses' that Lawrence Durrell

The rugged west coast near Paleokastritsa

found here still has its effect, perhaps best appreciated from the natural belvedere of the Bella Vista on the road above (see pp.141, 152).

Three of Paleokastritsa's coves (Agia Triada, Platakia and Alipa) form a cluster of beaches in the shape of a clover leaf which offer perfect bathing, particularly for families with young children. Each cove has a taverna and other facilities. Of the beaches, those nearer the monastery are sandiest, with some pebbles at the water's edge; further away they tend more to shingle. Water taxis and excursion boats line up to take swimmers to many other beaches on this stretch of coast, some of them lonely coves which are reachable by no other means. Snorkelling and skin-diving are rewarding, and a most comprehensive range of watersports is available in the resort, including a diving school. There are innumerable bars, restaurants (lobster is a local speciality), tourist shops, hotels, apartments and nightspots.

As you enter the village a turning to the left leads to the harbour (the land alongside part of the quay is the property of the Greek navy and photography is forbidden). From the quay beyond, boat excursions depart to the surrounding coves, the grottoes and the rock of Kolovri out to sea, which is yet another claimant to be identified with the *Odyssey*'s petrified Phaeacian ship. Continuing through the crowded tourist strip the road emerges between two small sandy beaches, where there is a bus stop and a mobile post office. From here a narrow road, with glorious views all along its length, climbs around the final headland towards a large parking area beside the entrance to the monastery.

Said to have been founded by a monk from Pagi in 1228, the monastery has been destroyed and rebuilt several times: in its present form it dates mainly from the seventeenth century. Inside is a small stone-flagged courtyard bordered by the church and, on the opposite side, the green-shuttered cells of the monks, now empty. Inside the church an elaborate painted ceiling features a wooden carving of the Tree of Life. The iconostasis is shaped like a Corfiot belfry with bells in the arches: icons include a George and the Dragon by Poulakis. There is a small museum, a room housing an ancient olive press and, from the terrace, incomparable views of the blue sea and the rugged coastline to the south, while behind soar the dramatic white and green slopes of Angelokastro (from which Paleokastritsa, 'the Old Castle', gets its name). Today only a single priest is usually on hand to receive the daily influx of visitors. The monastery is open from 07.00–13.00 and 15.00–20.00 between April and October. Visitors are requested not to enter unless respectfully dressed (i.e. not in swimming costumes); entrance is free but a donation to the offertory box is appreciated. A cannon near the monastery bears the eagles of the Russian Tsar.

To drink in the full majesty of the landscape, take the road that winds steeply uphill to Lakones from the outskirts, near the Paleo Disco. Better still, make the ascent on foot. Of several paths up, the best starts along a track opposite the taverna 'Calm' on the bend just before the Paleokastritsa town sign and the turning to the port. Ascend a steep track and keep right at the first fork, going steeply up past a few villas; then, just before the track becomes metalled and begins to descend again, a rough path leads off to the left; mica glints in the rock and scratched arrows help keep you on the track which soon bears right, becoming a mule path paved with rough stones which turn into shallow steps. The path continues upwards, mostly through the shade of laboriously terraced and well-netted olive groves, emerging after about half an hour on the main road in the centre of Lakones. Here turn left along the road, passing a small workshop producing items in carved olive wood, to reach the celebrated Bella Vista café. Here you can have a cool drink or a snack and absorb the breathtaking views of the monastery, the bays and coves of Paleokastritsa below you and, to the south, the wild headlands of the west coast embracing their secret beaches.

From here it is of course possible to continue northwards to Angelokastro, Ag. Georgiou Bay, etc., as described in Route 2. For the purposes of this tour, however, return along the road from Paleokastritsa to Corfu Town for 3 km, then turn right for **Liapades**. Follow signs to the village shortly afterwards, a substantial community with some handsome houses set on a low hill behind thick olive woods; just before you enter Liapades proper a profusion of signs directs you to the right, past a church. This leads to the beach, a pretty cove in a very picturesque setting beneath high limestone cliffs clothed in cypresses. The beach is coarse grey sand with pebbles which become larger rocks beyond the waterline. Unfortunately there is too much development in the vicinity for the size of the beach, which is often crowded; there are sunbeds, pedaloes, canoes and watersports; also boat trips to Paleokastritsa and the 'Blue Grotto' as well as other sand and pebble coves to the south which are only accessible from the sea.

Back on the main road turn right (there is a Shell petrol station nearby) along the flat Ropa Plain, one of Corfu's most fertile agricultural areas since the Italians drained it during their brief occupation in the early 1940s. A scenic minor road, set about with trees and bordered with a profusion of wild flowers in spring, branches off to the right after 2 km, passing through the pretty white-washed hamlets of Kanakades and Marmaro to make for the much larger settlement of Giannades. Set in a prominent position above the valley floor, this village's main square forms a natural balcony over the green meadows of the plain. After Giannades the minor road winds through lush country until it meets a T-junction, where a right turn leads down to the beach at **Ermones**. Backed by a steep hillside this is an 'afternoon beach', like many on the west coast. The beach, a mixture of fine brown shingle and rounded pebbles like sugared almonds, shelves quite steeply – it is ideal for swimmers but not so good for young children. Unhappily the setting is considerably spoilt by the bungalows of the Ermones Beach Hotel, for whose cosseted guests a funicular railway runs down from the top of the hill to the beach. Scuba diving features among the watersports available here.

The name of the Nausicaa restaurant behind the beach reminds us that the stream at Ermones cove is popularly identified with the river in which the Phaeacian princess was washing her clothes when Odysseus appeared, naked and salt-caked, from behind a bush after being washed up here the night before. Today the stream is still there, though it is hardly the 'noble river with never-failing pools' that Homer describes. But descriptions of the Ropa before the war indicate that the stream *was* quite fast-flowing before the drainage work undertaken by the Italians, so the idea is not entirely far-fetched.

The road inland from Ermones passes the entrance to Corfu's only golf course (see p.91), just before crossing a narrow bridge over the Ropa river. Immediately after this is the village of **Vatos**, set on the lower slopes of the isolated mountain of Agios Georgios (392 m). Vatos is a charming and tranquil village, full of picturesque corners and pots of flowers. A steep path up from the village affords stunning views of the Ropa plain and Ermones, while goat bells provide a timeless accompaniment.

South of Agios Georgios there is a string of splendid sandy beaches, only some of which have suffered development. The most northerly of these lies below the monastery of **Mirtiotissa** (Our Lady of the Myrtles), at the end of a rough and easily missed track signposted (not prominently and only in Greek) to the monastery. To find it, take the right fork when the road divides shortly after Vatos and start looking for the monastery sign about 1 km further on. Note that the track is very rutted, becoming steep and slippery nearer the coast, where it is unwise to attempt the final slither down to the beach even with four-wheel drive. The track is about 1½ km long and motorists give up at various stages depending on the capacity of their vehicle – when you do abandon the car please ensure it is sociably parked! The walk down is very pleasant, with good views. Mirtiotissa is lyrically described in *Prospero's Cell* – Lawrence Durrell called it 'perhaps the loveliest beach in the world' and praised its 'liongold sand'. While no longer the well-kept secret it once was, it is a delightful stretch of fine sand and crystal clear shallow water, backed by sheer cliffs from which fresh water oozes and trickles over the beach. On an eminence at the northern end of the beach the small white-washed monastery stands in a grove of olives, cypress and banana trees – rough paths lead up Agios Georgios from here. A section of the beach is (unofficially) nudist; there is excellent snorkelling from both ends. Unfortunately the beach (whose size varies considerably from year to year depending on the force of the winter storms) is often crowded – boat trips bring bathers from Paleokastritsa, Ermones and Glifada to add to those arriving by the road and on foot.

Back on the main road, still winding through olive groves, a turning to the right after 2 km leads to **Glifada** beach, a longer stretch of sand to which road access has been greatly improved in recent years – with the inevitable result that it is fast developing into a busy resort. Although about 1 km long and by no means narrow, Glifada's beach of golden sand becomes unpleasantly crowded in high season; but it remains an attractive setting, backed by steep hillsides and enclosed by rock formations at each end – the water is clean, without weeds or rocks and gets deep quite quickly after an initial ledge. (It should be noted that swimming conditions can be dangerous, however, as with many of these west coast beaches: a safety flag is sometimes hung – do not enter the sea if it is flying.) As well as sunbeds, pedaloes, etc., there is a full range of watersports, mostly run by the luxury Glyfada Beach Hotel which dominates the resort; at present there are also some two dozen villas, a beach bar and a couple of restaurants (one offering folk dancing and a disco in the evenings), but it seems unlikely that development will stop there.

From Glifada the road surface deteriorates as it climbs along a glorious corniche to the pleasantly airy village of **Pelekas**, built (like most sizeable villages on this side of the island) high up as a defence against seaborne raiders. Pelekas is popular with young people travelling independently, and is full of garish signs advertising *pensions* and small houses with rooms to let, as well as restaurants, discos, ticket agencies etc. – the place is already largely spoilt by tourism and new building is still going on. In the centre a church bizarrely houses a small supermarket under its truncated belfry: following the road round this church (signs read 'to the sunset') brings you past the school to a summit, where there is parking and, on the eastern side of the eminence, the so-called 'Kaiser's Throne'. This is a panoramic point (provided with a telescope) to which Kaiser Wilhelm II was fond of motoring from the Achilleion in order to watch the sunset. From the 'Throne' there are magnificent views of Mt Pantokrator to the north and a large tract of the eastern side of the island, including Corfu Town and the mainland uplands: south lies Agii Deka and the west coast, while looking seawards, Agios Georgios rears to the north-west and the coast can be seen far below. The sunsets from here are indeed memorable.

Descend back to the supermarket church and left through the village, emerging on a shady avenue which winds down to the main Ermones-Sinarades road: at the first hairpin bend out of the village a track leads down to Pelekas beach, another sandy and undeveloped stretch (apart from a scattering of tavernas in summer) where nudism is unofficially tolerated. At the road junction at the bottom of the hill (where going straight on would take you quickly back to Corfu Town only 10 km away), turn right, following signs for Sinarades and Lefkimmi. This road follows a tributary of the Potamos river: after about 3 km there is a steeply shelving pebbly beach, dominated by the large Yaliskari Palace Hotel, down a road to the right, and shortly after this the road begins to climb and you come to a fork. Here keep right to enter **Sinarades** (pop.1200), a picturesque huddle of flower-festooned houses along a narrow main street: most of the side streets are shallow flights of steps. Here a minor road leads down to a fine viewpoint at Plitiri Point, and up a lane to the right past the village centre is the Folk Museum, a preservation, complete with contents and decoration, of a nineteenth-century village house (200 dr.).

Continuing southwards, 1 km beyond Sinarades a turning to the right is signposted for **Agios Gordis**. This road descends steeply down a broom-covered hillside to a long beach with views of a splendid limestone stack at the far end. At the bottom there is a small (inadequate, in fact) area of parking where a little stream runs into the beach. Agios Gordis has a dramatically beautiful setting with thickly wooded hills behind and is not yet overdeveloped, but what building there has been is mostly piecemeal and unfortunate: on the hillside the number of villas is growing, while at beach level stands the large Agios Gordis Hotel and another, smaller hotel on a rocky outcrop at the opposite end; there

Agios Gordis

are very few (mostly unprepossessing) buildings in between as yet and no proper road. Vehicles tend to drive along the beach, which is a gently shelving expanse of light brown sand with some shingle and rocks at the water's edge, becoming more pebbly further north. There is a Diving Centre, and other watersports facilities including jet skis; the snorkelling and spear-fishing is good at each end of the beach, and boats can be hired.

Leave Agios Gordis and rejoin the road behind the resort which immediately climbs once again towards Kato Garouna 2 km further on. Here it bears left and just past the village an optional detour may be made by going straight on where the Corfu road bears left again. (This takes you down to the hillside village of Pentation, from which an unmetalled road follows the coast to Paramona, where there is a chapel and a taverna; there is also a rather seaweed-infested beach of changeable quality – depending on the force of winter storms the sand has been known to disappear altogether.) Less than 1 km after this bend, a second turning to the right (unsignposted) offers a second diversion southwards, to Agios Mattheos and the Byzantine castle at Gardiki.

This pretty road, metalled but narrow, skirts the Messonghi valley, passing Vouniatades with its vineyards and market gardens to reach the sizeable village of **Agios Mattheos** 2 km further on. Here the vine-hung houses climb the lower slopes of the small conical peak (463 m) which shares the village's name; the red-topped Venetian belfry stands out clearly against the wooded hillside. Our road skirts the eastern edge of the village along a road lined with maples, poplar and pavement cafes; a right turn off it from it leads to the coast at Paramona.

From the far end of village a fairly strenuous walk can be made up Mt. Agios Mattheos, through forests of kermes oak and other indigenous trees to the monastery near the summit (allow about 2 hours); there are superb almost vertical views from the top and you may see buzzards wheeling up here. The path commences just after the road crests a ridge and before the olive groves begin again (there is a shop here with an elaborate wayside shrine) – you will know you're on the correct track if you find yourself walking past a group of Snow White's dwarves in a garden beside you!

Ag. Mattheos is clearly bent on expansion: a sign announces the extent of the village just after this path, but almost 1 km further on there is a second set of signs. Here a metalled road goes to the right (signposted to the Villa Katerina bar): where it forks stand the ruins of **Gardiki** castle, constructed by the Despots of Epirus in the thirteenth century, though it is hard to understand why the builders of Angelokastro chose this low-lying site. Only the outer walls survive today, meeting at eight square postern towers: most of them, however, are still at their full height. The castle is used as an enclosure for cattle during the winter and is therefore abuzz with flies for much of the year – entrance can be gained by walking a little way along the left fork of the road, which leads on eventually to the northern end of Lake Korission at Mesavrisi. The right fork at this junction brings you to the southern slopes of the mountain, where a huge fire-blackened paleolithic cave was found which produced the oldest evidence of human life on Corfu (from around 40,000 BC). Also along this track are two beaches, the second of which, Sidi Beach, is long, sandy and usually completely deserted.

After this diversion there are two possible routes back to Corfu Town: either continue south for 2 km to the bridge over the Messonghi where you can join the main Lefkimmi-Corfu coastal road (as Route 4); or return the way you came, turning right after about 7 km when you meet the road from Kato Garouna.

The road now climbs the western slopes of Agii Deka and runs along a shady shelf through spectacular mountain scenery. A no through road to the right leads still higher – to the perched village of Ano Garouna: cars cannot enter the village, but one can walk through it to reach the abandoned monastery set in a small plateau of lush vegetation and fruit trees that lies at the top of the mountain. After this the road descends through dense woods, eventually joining the main Sinarades-Corfu road near Kastellani, where a right turn takes you past Kinopiastes and brings you back into town past Gastouri and through Vrioni as described at the beginning of Route 4.

TOURING CORFU

4: *The South*

Even the most hurried tour of southern Corfu will occupy a full day, and if the area is explored with all the possible diversions more than two days would probably be required – visitors based south of Corfu Town, of course, will find it easier to explore this undervalued part of the island at more leisure. Some of the detours below will appeal to beach-fanciers, others to botanists or lovers of scenery: there is something for everyone in southern Corfu. It is probably not practical to incorporate more than two detours into a single day's touring – it is up to you to pick from the various options described.

Leave Corfu Town from San Rocco Square via Don. Dimoulitsa Street, following signs for the airport, Benitses and Lefkimmi. Shortly you will find yourself veering right and passing the end of the airport runway (a stretch of road that is briefly closed when wind conditions compel the airliners to take off southwards, so close is the runway to the road), before skirting the Chalikiopoulos lagoon. The route out of town passes through some unattractive suburbs (with the occasional leather or ceramics showroom by the road) and a row of market gardens on the shores of the lagoon: some of these are still owned by the descendants of Maltese immigrants encouraged by the British to settle here in the nineteenth century – tomatoes, vegetables, grapes, melons, strawberries and citrus fruits are the main crops.

Some 5 km south of Corfu Town there is a junction at Vrioni, a crafts centre, where there are workshops making ceramics, leather goods and items in brass and copper; here a left turn leads to Perama at the mouth of the lagoon and the main coastal road south. Our route, however, carries straight on (following signs to the Achilleion and Lefkimmi) and rapidly leaves the suburbs behind. After 3 km a turning to the left leads to the large village of Gastouri, locally famous for its dancing and for the beauty of its womenfolk, who traditionally wore their hair piled high. The Achilleion lies 2 km up this leafy road, should you wish to combine a visit with this route.

Condemned by Henry Moore as 'an abomination in the face of

nature and all things lovely' and by Lawrence Durrell as 'a monstrous building surrounded by gimcrack sculptures', the **Achilleion** is nevertheless one of the most visited sites in Corfu. Coach parties arrive constantly to view this tasteless and grotesquely ornate pleasure palace, which was built for the beautiful, melancholy Empress Elizabeth of Austria ('Sissy'), wife of Franz Josef. Elizabeth sought to find on Corfu a tranquil refuge from the intrigues of the Hapsburg court and in the early 1890s ordered the construction of a summer palace on a hillside near Gastouri which was to be 'worthy of Achilles'. Unfortunately her Italian architects produced a pretentious, ill-proportioned, pseudo-classical building, decorated inside in a heavily Victorian version of the 'Pompeian style'.

Unhappy Elizabeth was assassinated by an Italian anarchist in 1898 and the Achilleion remained empty for some years, until in 1907 it was purchased by Kaiser Wilhelm II: he brought his entire entourage to the palace every year from 1908 to 1914, and had a jetty and the 'Kaiser's Bridge' constructed on the coast below so that he could step straight on to his land from the Royal yacht. Used as a military hospital during the First War, the Achilleion became the property of the Greek government until, highly appropriately, the opulently decorated upper floors were converted into a casino in 1962. The building was also used as one of the exotic settings for the James Bond film *For Your Eyes Only*.

The lower floor and the gardens are open to the public. Passing under the massive pillars of the portico, the visitor enters an enormous hall with a painted ceiling and grand staircase dominated by a large mural (the work of the Austrian painter Franz Mats) depicting the triumphant Achilles dragging the body of Hector behind his chariot. Around the hall are a small chapel and rooms containing original furnishings and memorabilia of the Empress and the Kaiser. Exhibits include a large Winterhalter portrait of Elizabeth, photographs and documents and – always an object of particular interest – the curious saddle seat which the Kaiser favoured for writing at his desk.

Outside, the beauty of the extensive gardens and the magnificent panoramic views from the grounds more than compensates for the Achilleion's architectural infelicities. Among a mass of bougainvillea, wistaria, palms and roses stand many pieces of statuary of indifferent quality – the best is a bronze of the dying Achilles by the German sculptor Ernst Herter, now rather discoloured by the winter rains. Overlooking the glorious view from the end of the garden is a standing figure of the hero, 8 m high, so placed that it cannot be seen properly from any direction. This was erected by the Kaiser, who had it inscribed 'to the greatest of Greeks from the greatest of Germans'. Beside the palace the 'terrace of the Muses' is crowded with more statues, some of them copies of originals in

Dying Achilles in the gardens of the Achilleion

the gardens of the Villa Borghese. The Achilleion is open from 08.00–19.00 daily (admission 250 dr.). Opposite the entrance is the Vassilakis distillery, offering wine, spirit and liqueur tasting.

From the Gastouri turning follow signs for Agios Gordis for a further few hundred metres, where there is an almost obliterated sign to the right for **Kinopiastes**, a quiet hill village. As well as the celebrated Tripa taverna (see p.32), there is a monastery here, with stunning views of the surrounding country.

From the Kinopiastes road it is not far to the next turning, this time to the left and signposted Agii Deka; take this road, which hairpins up the opposite side of the valley with glorious views extending past the Achilleion and Gastouri right over to Corfu Town and the Greek coast. Ten minutes later the straggle of houses that is the village of Agii Deka appears above the road: its name, 'Ten Saints', commemorates a group of Cretan Christians, soldiers in the Roman army, who were martyred for their faith. From it a path leads up to a plateau between the two peaks of the mountain (576 m) after which the village is named: here, amidst a mass of wild flowers, there is an unexpected area of cultivated land and an abandoned monastery. Below the road the slope is now almost sheer: soon you are looking down onto the seaside resort of Benitses (for walkers, there is a steep path down to the coast here, which passes the old British waterworks, see pp.73–4). Other traditional and unspoilt hill villages accessible from this road include Stavros and Dafnata, reached up a turning 3 km from Agii Deka: both contain many charming old houses and enjoy magnificent views.

After the Stavros turning the road descends more gently into the fertile valley of the Messonghi river, full of olive groves and market gardens, eventually reaching the straggling village of Strongili. On the valley floor there is more market gardening as well as sheep farming and a few small vineyards. It is a landscape of peaceful rurality, ablaze with wild flowers in the spring and completely unaffected by tourism.

About 12 km from Agii Deka this quiet road meets the main west coast road from Corfu Town. Turn right onto this (i.e. straight on) and cross the Messonghi bridge. (There is a Mobil petrol station here.) From the bridge the road is broad, well-surfaced and mainly level, with occasional glimpses of Lake Korission beginning to appear on the right. At the small village of Linia (petrol station), 6 km from the bridge, two possible diversions present themselves, one to Issos beach and Lake Korission, the other to the hill town of Chlomos:

At the far end of the village a patchily metalled road to the right (signposted) leads down through vineyards and fields of potatoes and artichokes to **Issos Beach,** ten minutes away, a broad, wild and immensely long strip of tawny soft sand backed by dunes that stretches as far as the eye can see. There is no shade on the beach, still less any beach facilities, and weed and flotsam pile up in places; but the water shelves gently and Issos offers near-perfect bathing – its sheer size means it is never crowded. It is possible to walk its entire length and ultimately skirt **Lake Korission** on the seaward side. More interestingly, scramble up the dunes behind the beach at any point to make your way towards the lake. This large expanse of shallow water almost dries up in summer; grey mullet used to be farmed in the lake for taramasalata (produced from their roe), and duck-shooting is popular here in the autumn. The water's edge is reached from Issos beach across a wild area of dunes which offers much to interest the botanist, who will be absorbed by the innumerable small flowering plant species, the spurges, occasional orchids, sea rocket, sea stock and many other sand-loving species. Among large tussocks of marram grass and small groves of trees large Balkan green lizards abound, tortoises can be seen and, in winter, water birds of all kinds frequent the lake shore – ducks, avocets, stilts, herons of several varieties and many types of wader among them. It is an unexpected landscape to find in Corfu, and one in which one can wander around for a long time without exhausting its fascination. Offshore lie two small islets, the Lagoudia Islands: traces of Roman villas have been found on them, suggesting the islands were once larger than they are today.

Back at Linia it is also possible to turn inland and climb the most southerly range of hills on the island (380m):

> Follow signs for Chlomos up a steep and hairpinning ascent offering broad views of Lake Korission and the south-west coast. At the top of the ridge there are equally fine panoramic views of the other side of the island, and also of Paxos and the Greek mainland. The large village of **Chlomos** itself is a tumbling huddle of grey roofs around a maze of narrow alleys. From it a track leads to the pretty village of Kouspades and a number of small fishing villages on the east coast (also accessible from Argirades, see below); northwards a road through the village of Spilio would take you to Messongi and the main coast road back to town.

From Linia continue south on the main road for a further 1

Argirades monastery

km, where a metalled road to the right (well signposted) leads to the growing tourist development of **Agios Georgios**, the most popular resort in the south-western part of Corfu.

Pinewoods and groves of gigantic olive trees back the beach here, which is strictly a section of the enormous sandy strip stretching from Maga Choro point to the northern end of Lake Korission – a distance of almost 12 km. The resort (not to be confused with the northern beach of the same name) sprawls rather haphazardly along a more rocky stretch between the southern end of Issos beach and the so-called 'Golden Beach' to the south, which is narrower, more steeply shelving and backed by low scrubby cliffs: facilities here include sunbeds and umbrellas, pedaloes, canoes, windsurfing and other watersports and some boat trips. Between these are villas, bars, tavernas and a public swimming pool, widely spaced and set down apparently at random – producing a somewhat unlovely effect. In recent years the resort has experienced problems with both its water and its electricity supplies.

Just under 3 km from Linia lies the substantial village of Argirades, the first intimation of which is the magnificent Venetian belfry of its monastery to the right of the road as you approach the outskirts.

From Argirades a pleasant excursion northwards may be made to a group of villages near the east coast – Kouspades, Boukari, Korakades and Petreti. This road runs through intensely cultivated land past Neochoraki to the extremely pretty mountain hamlet of **Kouspades** ($2\frac{1}{2}$ km), its gleaming white houses covered with vine trellises; beyond it lies the quiet fishing village of Boukari with two tavernas and some small hotels, and up a turning to the right just outside Kouspades the attractive partially deserted village of Korakades. At Petreti, another fishing village 2 km to the east, there is a mud-flat beach, also with a taverna; the ruins of a Roman bathhouse have been found nearby.

Perivolion, 4 km down the road from Argirades, is a cluster of generally dilapidated buildings around a prominent church. Northwards a road leads to the coast at Kaliviotes ($1\frac{1}{2}$ km), where the beach, though attractively set, is largely rocky; in the other direction a sign 'To the Beach' by the church leads via a road (shown as a track on most maps but now metalled for part of its length) through vineyards and groves of orange and olive trees to the entirely new resort of **Santa Barbara** ($2\frac{1}{2}$ km) at the southern end of the long strip of sand which began at Lake Korission. Santa Barbara, isolated and lacking public transport, is pleasingly undeveloped as yet; the beach of reddish gold sand is excellent and there are a few restaurants, a scattering of villas and minimal beach facilities – the beach is popular with windsurfers. There was nothing here at all a few years ago.

South of Perivolion there is a BP petrol station and 3 km further on Lefkimmi is reached. The 'capital' of southern Corfu is really a succession of linked villages, which act as the centre of a self-sufficient, untouristic (and therefore often extremely visitor-friendly), working agricultural region where the traditional Corfiot way of life is still preserved with women riding donkeys much in evidence and pretty circular haystacks in the fields. This area is also the centre of wine production on Corfu. From Ano Lefkimmi, the first of these villages, a road to the left leads to the extensive saltpans at Alikes and the tip of Cape Lefkimmi, scene of the first great naval battle in history, when the Corcyraeans beat the Corinthians in 664 BC: the landscape however, is not picturesque and the excursion scarcely worth making. Instead follow the road through Lefkimmi, past several sizeable churches of varying quality, to Potami where a bailey bridge crosses the Chimaros river – a surprisingly wide stream, filled with caiques moored along its banks like a miniature Amsterdam. To the left an unmetalled track leads to a small beach at **Bouka**, with gently shelving, fine powdery sand and crystal-clear water; usually deserted, Bouka makes a refreshing contrast to the teeming sands of Kavos, a few km to the south.

From here the road continues southwards, reaching **Kavos** after 6½ km. This crowded, unsophisticated and fast-growing resort, especially incongruous in this rural and remote corner of the island, lies at the end of an enormous

View from the bridge, Potami

(if narrow) beach separated from the road by a belt of trees. Despite its isolation from the rest of the island, Kavos has mushroomed disastrously in recent years and is dusty with continuous construction work. In the early months of the season it is especially popular with families with young children, who enjoy the sandy beach and the very shallow water. In July and August, however, it attracts young people and is often rowdy (there are no police in Kavos, and to some extent the local authorities regard it as a 'no-go area' best left to itself). The resort offers a proliferation of bars, restaurants, gift shops and discos, some of the less obtrusive of them set amongst the trees behind the beach, where you may spot such establishments as the 'Fort Bliss cocktail bar' and the 'Fawlty Towers' apartments – there is nothing Greek about Kavos. The beach itself, though narrow and seaweed-covered in patches, stretches almost as far as the eye can see. It is composed of pale soft sand and shelves extremely gently: long jetties run out at intervals but the water may be only knee-deep even at the end of them. There is a comprehensive range of watersports available and a variety of boat excursions – to Paxos and Antipaxos and several spots on the mainland, especially Parga. Both the resort and the beach are unpleasantly overcrowded during the tourist season.

Kavos offers little (beyond an overpriced drink and perhaps a swim) to visitors interested in the real Corfu. However a popular walk from the resort to Cape Asprokavos, the southern tip of the island, is almost irresistible now that one has come so far (allow about 40 minutes each way).

Drive through the centre of Kavos and continue as far as you can (past the bus stop); eventually the road turns back on itself for Spartero (shortly after which it becomes too rough to be attempted in an ordinary car). Park here and enter the olive groves near the sign which announces the end of Kavos, bearing right and ignoring turnings to the left. In no time you are in peaceful countryside walking along a track lined with wild flowers in spring and heather and cistus in later months. After about half an hour, ignore a minor fork to the left. The trees, kermes oak, myrtle and mastic, grow so straight that it is hard to believe the coast is anywhere near, yet shortly after this a gap on your left will make you suddenly aware that you are right at the tip of the island: pale sandy cliffs plunge down to a narrow beach of dark sand below you and Paxos is clearly visible slightly to the left. A few minutes later the monastery of Panagia Arkoudillas comes into view, its early eighteenth-century belfry set among tall cypresses festooned with hanging creepers: one of the buildings is a complete ruin while the chapel is sadly decayed and hastening to join it – inside a few

The ruined monastery of Panagia Arkoudillas on Cape Asprokavos

pews remain intact. The steps leading to the upper floor stop 3 metres from the entrance – clearly a plank was used to bridge the gap, which could be removed if pirates landed on the coast near this scenic but remote spot. Depending on tree-thinning work you may be able to scramble up the hillside behind the monastery, an effort rewarded by a fine view of the lovely beach of Arkoudillas to the west. (The beach cannot, however, be reached from here – see below.) Return from the cape by the same route: as you descend through the peace of the olive groves – many of the trees are so huge they may have been planted in Venetian times – the only sound will be a goat or a donkey tearing at the grass, making the approach to the tourist hubbub of Kavos even more of a shock.

Unfortunately, the condition of the road between Kavos and Spartero at present makes a circular tour of the southern tip of Corfu impracticable for anyone without four-wheel drive or a very strong motorcycle. Arkoudillas beach can be reached on foot by continuing from the end of the metalled road just outside Kavos, which will take you through Spartero to Dragotina in approx. 1 hour; here a path leads to the coast at Kanula, where a left turn and a little scrambling bring you to the beach, which is large, clean, sandy with some strangely shaped rocks, backed by spectacular cliffs – and usually completely deserted. (The track at Dragotina can also be reached on a rough road from Lefkimmi, going right from the prominent church of Ag. Arsenios via Bastatika and Neochorion, but in a single day you are unlikely to have time to combine this diversion with any other touring in southern Corfu unless you are already staying in or near this section of the island.)

Return from Kavos, therefore, threading your way through the thronging streets of the resort before heading back up the island towards the Messonghi bridge. Here there are several alternative routes back to Corfu Town: straight on is our earlier road, via Agii Deka and Strongili; to the left a scenic road (described on pp.156-7) goes north through Agios Mattheos and the western slopes of Agii Deka. To complete the southern route, however, follow the main road right at the bridge and back up the east coast to the capital.

Messongi, at the mouth of the river of the same name, lies a little off the main road, which turns north here to follow the coast. The remains of Greek temples have been found in the hills near the village, and Messongi boasts some of the largest olive trees on the island, said to be 700 years old and originally planted when the Venetians first introduced the trees as the island's main crop. The river Messonghi, in full flow even in high summer, makes the area fertile, but the terrain here is still fairly flat; consequently both Messongi and nearby **Moraitika** have suffered from the building of several large hotels and a wide strip of development behind a long narrow beach of pebbly coarse sand. Of the two, Messongi is the more attractive and retains a village atmosphere with a picturesque waterfront: there is the usual range of beach and watersport facilities including scuba-diving. The resort is dominated by the 1587-bed Messonghi Beach Hotel, which is patronised almost exclusively by British visitors. Moraitika, on the other side of the river, is somewhat more commercial, with many hotels, tavernas and bars: the beach, reached by a narrow track through orchards, is a long strip of coarse sand, with pebbles at the water's edge. On the outskirts of the settlement, opposite the BP service station, the remains of a Roman villa and bath have been excavated.

Continuing north, the landscape becomes more mountainous, with occasional small beaches (and one longer, man-made one). Pleasant-looking villas dot the steep wooded hillsides on the inland side of the road, until, some 7 km north of Moraitika, the road descends to sea level at **Benitses**. Once a small fishing village with a minimal beach nestling in tranquillity beneath the wrinkled slopes of Agii Deka, this resort has in recent years become infamous as an example of unbridled touristic exploitation, a reputation which the fatal knifing of a tourist in 1988 has done little to improve. Benitses has a small, mostly man-made beach of gritty pebbles, but its main 'attraction' is its lively nightlife, which appeals to a young, noisy (and occasionally violent) clientèle. The tourist strip is set back from the main road and consists of a characterless line of bars, restaurants and discos, which function rowdily into the small hours and beyond.

Traces of a more civilized era remain in Benitses, however. There are a few older cottages still visible, and in the rear garden of a house at the northern end of the resort the remains of a Roman bath house with some surviving floor mosaics can be seen. Behind the village cemetery a steep path leads up the mountain towards Stavros, past the waterworks built by the second British Lord High Commissioner, Sir Frederick Adam, in the 1820s: the aqueduct to which they were linked has gone, but the perpetual spring up here still provides the water for much of the immediate area.

Leave Benitses, passing the Shell Museum (open 09.00–17.00 daily) on the left. Shortly afterwards a shady road to the left climbs steeply through the olive groves to the Achilleion (see pp.158–60). Just after the Achilleion turning the demolished remains of the so-called **Kaiser's Bridge** stand beside the road next to a dilapidated pier: when Kaiser Wilhelm II visited the Achilleion it was his custom to disembark here and cross the road via the bridge to reach his estate.

From here the road ascends to a corniche before reaching **Perama**, a scattered community of villas set in gardens overflowing with bougainvillea and wistaria which climb the hillside overlooking the sea and the celebrated Mouse Island. The first home of the Durrell family when they came to Corfu, the 'small strawberry-pink villa, like some exotic fruit lying in the greenery', was at Perama, which still has more of the feel of an elegant residential suburb than a resort, though nowadays the proximity of the airport inevitably detracts from its peace. There are small pebbly man-made beaches reached by steps at the bottom of the slope, but they are unlikely to attract non-residents. Perama also has a number of nightclubs and discos, which draw clients from Corfu Town. An unmarked path by the Restaurant Pierotto near the bend at the far end of Perama leads down to the causeway by which pedestrians and cyclists can cross the mouth of the Chalikiopoulos lagoon to the tip of the Kanoni peninsula and the Vlacherna convent (see also p.125).

After Perama the road turns inland to skirt the lagoon once again, joining the main road out of Corfu Town at Vrioni after 2 km. Here turn right and return through the outskirts of town, negotiating the hair-raisingly uncontrolled left fork opposite the airport to reach San Rocco Square.

Preparing for take-off below the balcony of the Royal Hotel; between flights, herons flap lazily about the lagoon

FURTHER READING

Chaitow, Alkmini, *Greek Vegetarian Cooking* (n.e. London, 1991)

Chatto, J., and Martin, W.L., *A Kitchen in Corfu* (London, 1987)

Dicks, Brian, *Corfu* (Newton Abbot, 1977)

Durrell, Lawrence, *Prospero's Cell* (London, 1945)

Durrell, Gerald, *My Family and Other Animals* (London, 1956)

Foss, Arthur, *The Ionian Islands* (London, 1969)

Hart, Sir B. Liddell (ed.), *Letters of Private Wheeler 1809–28* (London, 1952)

Heinzel, H., Fitter, R., and Parslow, J., *The Birds of Britain and Europe* (London, 1972)

Homer, *The Odyssey* (tr. Rieu) (London, 1946)

Hopkins, Margaret, *Corfu* (London, 1977)

Huxley, A., and Taylor, W., *Flowers of Greece and the Aegean* (London, 1977)

Jervis-White-Jervis, H., *The Ionian Islands During the Present Century* (London, 1863)

Joinville, Jean de, and Villehardouin, Geoffrey de, *Chronicles of the Crusades* (tr. Shaw) (London, 1969)

Lear, *Selected Letters* (ed. V. Noakes) (Oxford, 1988)

Lear, Edward, *Views in the Seven Ionian Islands* (London, 1863)

Morris, Jan, *The Venetian Empire: A Sea Voyage* (London 1980)

Paipetis, H.W., *Corfu Book of Walks* (Corfu, 1987)

Polunin, Oleg, *Trees and Bushes of Britain and Europe* (Oxford 1976)

Rochford, N., *Landscapes of Corfu* (London, 1987)

Stewart, Mary, *This Rough Magic* (London, 1970)

Thucydides, *History of the Peloponnesian War* (tr. Warner) (London, 1954)

INDEX AND GAZETTEER

(Figures in brackets after place name entries indicate distance in km from Corfu Town with approximate direction)

beach on Cape Varvara 133, 134

Avliotes (28 NW) large agricultural village on Ag. Stefanos–Sidari road 146

banks 4, 35–6

Barbati (11 NNW) small E coast resort at foot of high cliffs, S of Nissaki 18, 43, 63, 130

Benitses (8 S) lively E coast resort, manmade beach, rowdy nightlife; Shell Museum, remains of Roman villa and British waterworks 3, 14, 20, 21, 32, 43, 67, 73, 78, 90, 97, 100, 158, 160, 168

bicycles 9, 101

birds 56–60, 92, 96, 101, 136, 157, 161

boat hire 128, 130, 134, 144, 156

boat excursions 99–103, **99**, 130, 132, 134, 147, 151, 152, 163, 165

Bouka (26 SE) quiet sandy beach 1 km downstream from Potami 164

Boukari (20 SSE) fishing hamlet on W side of bay of Lefkimmi 21, 163

British 25, 72–5, 80, 83, 90, 110, 112, 113, 114, 115, 121, 122, 140, 158, 160

buses 4, 5, 13–14, 94, 101, 111, 151

butterflies 62–3, 136

Byzantium (Constantinople) 67–8, 70, 72, 80, 85, 87, 101, 105, 114, 119

camping 21–2

canoeing 90, 147, 152, 163

car hire 8–9, 11, 101

casino 34, 159

Cefalonia 43, 64, 68, 74, 103

cemetery, British 121–2

ceramics 105–6, 158

Chalikiopoulos lagoon (3 S)

shallow arm of the sea between Perama and Kanoni; main harbour of ancient Corcyra, now the site of Corfu airport 3, 32, 43, 57, 65, 78, 124, 158, **169**, 169

Chlomos (19 SSE) peaceful inland village on high ground in S Corfu 27, 161, 162

Christianity 64, 67, 101, 123

church services 42

cinemas 34

climate 40, 44–6, 56, 93, 97

coach excursions 97–8, 124, 138, 159

Comnenus, Michael Angelos 68, 141

consulates 41

Corcyra (classical name for Corfu) 26, 65–7, 85, 122, 123, 124, 164

'Corfu Incident' 76, 122

Corfu News 39, 41

Corfu Town (pop. 40,000) 1, 8, 10–17 *passim*, **12**, 29–31, **30**, 32–43 *passim*, 54, 56, 58, 60, 69–76 *passim*, 84, 86, 89, 92, 93, 94, 95, 97, 98–106 *passim*, 110–22, **120**, 126, 127, 129, 139, 140, 141, 142, 147, 148, 149, 155, 157, 158, 169

Corinth 66, 85, 133, 164

credit cards 36

Crete 68, 71, 80, 81

cricket 1, 75, 90, **90**, 114

cruises 5–6

cuisine, Corfiot 22–6, 29, 30, 31, 32, 55

culture 71, 72, 73, 80–4, 114

currency 4, 35–6

Cyprus 69, 86

Dafnata (10 S) quiet hill village on S side of Agii Deka 160

Dafni (22 NW) village inland from Ag. Georgiou beach; panoramic views, citrus trees, vineyards 144

Kapareli (19 NNE) rock in mid-channel between Corfu and Albania; lighthouse 134

Kapodistrias, Count John 72, 75, 82, 94, 112, 115, 121

Kardaki (2 S) ancient spring rediscovered during excavations of Temple of Apollo at Mon Repos 40, 66, 124

Karoussades (23 NW) large village inland from N coast; 16th-century church and Venetian houses 12, 22, 37, 147, 148

Kassiopi (18 N) fishing harbour and lively but unspoilt resort; small beaches, 13th-century castle, boat service to Corfu Town 12, 19, 31, 37, 38, 67, 80, 92, 97, 99, 103, 106, 126, 131, 133–4, **134**, 135, 148

Kastellani (8 SW) peaceful inland village off road between Corfu Town and Sinarades 37, 38, 157

Kato Garouna (11 SW) hill village inland from Agios Gordis 156, 157

Kato Korakiana (11 NW) attractive residential village in hills inland from Dasia 129

Kavadades (25 NW) sprawling village on ridge near Magoulades 22, 144

Kavos (30 SE) large, brash resort at southern tip of Corfu; fine sand, watersports facilities, uncontrolled night life 12, 21, 32, 33, 92, 94, 98, 99, 100, 164–6, 167

Kendroma (13 N) hill village with associated beach between Nissaki and Kalami 131

Kerasia (15 NNE) quiet E coast beach reachable on foot from Agios Stefanos 133

Kerkyra *see* Corfu

Kinopiastes (7 SW) picturesque hill village to W of Gastouri; monastery, Tripa taverna 32, 33, 97, 157, 160

Kompitsi (5 SW) tranquil hillside village off Pelekas road, imposing monastery, pleasant views

Kommeno (7 NW) E coast cape dividing Dafnila and Gouvia bays 17, 18, 31, 97, 99, 128, 129

Kontokali (6 WNW) minor E coast resort; pebbly beach, youth hostel 14, 17, 19, 22, 31, 92, 99, 105, 127, 128, 140

Korakades (19 SSE) partially decayed village N of Argirades 163

Korakiana (14 NW) large hill village 5 km inland from Pyrgi 149

Korission, Lake (20 S) large salt-water lagoon behind coastal sand dunes to N of Ag. Georgios 23, 43, 56, 57, **61**, 63, 157, 161, 162, 163

Kouloura (13 N) small, picturesque natural harbour on E coast, NE of Kalami 130, 131

koumkouats 24–5, 26, 78, 106, 140

Kouspades (20 SSE) pretty whitewashed village N of Argirades 162, 163

Koyevinas (18 N) large, little-visited stony beach near Cape Varvara; windsurfing 133

Krini (21 WNW) small village W of Lakones; starting point for walk to Angelokastro 27, 141, 142

Kritika (28 SE) remote, pretty village in extreme S

lace 106

Lagoudia islands (23 S) two islets off Issos beach 161

125, 158, 168-9

Perithia (Old) (16 NNW) almost deserted village nestling into N flank of Mt Pantokrator 54, 80, 126, 135-6, **135**

Perivolion (24 SSE) inland southern village with large church; access to Santa Barbara beach 12, 163, 164

Peroulades (28 NW) quiet village with two beaches S of Cape Drastis; interesting strata on cliffs 44, 146, 147

Petalia (16 NNW) wine-producing village on W side of Mt Pantokrator; access road to summit 27, 137, 138

Petreti (20 SSE) fishing village on W side of Lefkimmi Bay; Roman remains 163

petrol 8, 11-12

pharmacies 38-9

Philip, Prince, Duke of Edinburgh 73, 123

piracy 68, 69, 110, 135, 150, 166

Plataria mainland fishing village in beautiful bay visited by Corfu boat trips 100, 103

Platitera convent in outskirts of Corfu Town; paintings by many Cretan and Ionian artists and Kapodistrias' tomb 121

police 11, 16, 28, 35, 41, 42, 92, 113, 165

Pontokonissi (4 S) islet with chapel near mouth of Chalikiopoulos lagoon; popularly known as 'Mouse Island' 32, 65, 97, 99, 122, 125, **125**, 168

population 66, 77, 100, 142

postal services 4, 36, 37, 151

Potami (26 SE) continuation of Lefkimmi to the E 164, **164**

Potamos (4 W) inland town

and river N of capital 14, 44, 71, 74, 78, 80, 126, 155

Prinilas (21 NW) remote hamlet above Ag. Georgiou Bay 142, 143, 144

public holidays 36-7, 86-9

Pyrgi (11 NW) popular beach resort adjoining Ipsos; watersports, nightlife 13, 18, 19, 22, 32, 92, 97, 126, 129, 131, 137, 139

radio 40, 45, 93

reptiles 61-2, **61**, 96, 161

restaurants 23, 27-32, **28**, 97-8, 105, 112, 121, 125, 134, 141, 151, 152, 160

riding 92, 126

Roda (22 NW) resort village, cape and long sandy beach on N coast 12, 19, 22, 66, 85, 94, 103, 137, 140, 142, 147, 148

Romans 66, 67, 69, 110, 133, 143, 160, 161, 163, 168

Ropa river and plain area of fertile pasture land to S of Mt Arakli; golf course 43, 56, 59, 76, 78, **79**, 91, 149, 152, 153

Russians 72, 112, 119, 126

sailing 92, **93**, 128, 132

Santa Barbara (25 SSE) newly developing resort on sandy beach S of Perivolion 163-4

Schulenberg, Count John Matthias von der 70, 71, 114

Serbs 75-6, 112

Sfakera (20 NW) small inland village S of Roda 149

Sgombou (10 NW) road junction and hamlet between Tsavros and Paleokastritsa 106, 149

Shakespeare 2, 26

shopping 1, 98, 104-7, **104**, **106**, 116, 118, 120, **120**

Sicily 65, 66, 69
Sidari (26 NW) family resort on N coast; large sandy beach
shallow sea, rock formations 12, 19, 38, 44, 64, 85, 90, 94, 98, 100, 102, 103, 140, 142, 146, 147, 148
Sinarades (9 SW) large, pretty village with stepped streets; folk museum 20, 27, 155, 157
Sinies (14 NNW) abandoned mountain village on E flank of Mt Pantokrator, once famous for its quarries 118, 131
sizes (clothing) 107
Skidi (16 SSW) little visited sandy beach N of Lake Korission 157
Skripero (15 NW) inland village S of Mt Arakli range; views, old buildings 37, 149
snakes 39, 62, 96
Solomos, Dionysios 82, 84, 86, 112
'Sound and Light' 33, 34, 115
Spartero (31 SE) small inland village near southernpost tip of Corfu 165, 167
Spartilas (13 NW) mountain village on SW slope of Mt Pantokrator; colourful buildings and superlative views 130, 137, 138, 149
Spilio (18 S) scattered hill village between Messongi and Chlomos 162
Spiridon, Saint 67, 70, 71, 77, 86–7, 88, 119, 133
sports 90–7
Stavros (10 S) unspoilt hill village S of Agii Deka 160, 168
Strinilas (15 NNW) wine-producing village on W flank of Mt Pantokrator 27, 97, 130, 137, 138
Strongili (13 S) sprawling agricultural village on E side of Messonghi river 161

swimming 94–5, 112, 122, 147, 151, 153, 154, 163

taxis 4, 12–13, 101
telephones 37–8
tennis 95
Theotokis family 82, 119, 148
time differences 35
tipping 28, 39
tourism 1, 76, 79, 155, 168
Tourist Offices 16, 35, 41, 84, 90, 94, 98, 113
trees 53–6, 112, 115, 133, 134, 163, 165
Troumpeta (18 NW) mountain pass in Arakli range; excellent views 43, 140, 142, 147, 149
Tsavros (8 NW) road junction and hamlet N of Gouvia 33, 128, 140, 149, 150
Turks 45, 70, 71, 72, 74, 75, 80, 87, 112, 114, 118, 119, 120, 126, 127

Varvara, Cape (18 N) remote headland of Kassiopi; pebble beaches 133
Vatonies (19 NW) small village, half-hidden by orchards behind Ag. Georgiou Bay 143
Vatos (11 W) pretty, flowery village overlooking Ropa Plain 12, 22, **89**, 153
Venetians 22, 26, 27, 29, 66, 68–71, 77, 80, 82, 101, 103, 105, 110, 112, 114, 115, 118, 120, 124, 128, 129, 131, 133, 137, 166, 167
Vidos (2 N) strategic island off Corfu Town; once a prison and cemetery now a picnic spot, boats from Old Port 30, 76, 99, 112, 127, 129
Vistonas (21 WNW) inland village N of Paleokastritsa 142
Vlacherna (3 S) tiny convent with jewel-like interior lying

in water at S tip of Kanoni
peninsula 125, 169
Vouniatades (13 SSW)
agricultural village N of Ag.
Mattheos 156
Voutoumi beach and beauty
spot in Antipaxos 102
Vrikes sandy beach on E coast
of Antipaxos 102
Vrioni (5 SW) crafts centre
where roads from the capital
to Perama and Gastouri
diverge 157, 158, 169

walking 95–7, 101, 131, 135,
138, 141, 145, 156–7, 160,
167, 168

water 21, 25, 40, 45, 73–4, 100,
102, 114, 160, 163, 168
water-skiing 97, 128, 129
Wilhelm II 75, 155, 159, 168
windsurfing 96, 97, 102, 129,
133, 144, 146, 163, 164
wine 26, 26–7, 29, 69, 102, 106,
138, 141, 160, 164
World War II 76, 78, 87, 110,
111, 116, 117, 118, 124, 152

youth hostel 22
Yugoslavia 76

Zakynthos (Zante) 3, 43, 64,
82, 119